Advertising and Multilingual Repertoires

"In *Advertising and Multilingual Repertoires*, Marco Santello proposes a new theoretical framework for analyzing multilingualism and advertising that draws on both marketing principles and sociolinguistics. This volume includes an extensive review of the literature on multilingual advertising campaigns as well as effective linguistic strategies used in advertising targeting multilinguals."

Elizabeth Martin, *California State University, San Bernadino, USA*

Advertising and Multilingual Repertoires explores advertising from the perspective of multilingual audiences. Santello introduces the linguistic processes involved in advertising discourse, and analyses the relationship between the linguistic repertoires of audiences and language use in advertising.

This book:

- showcases the most recent advancements in linguistic research as applied to the study of advertising and multilingualism, adopting an approach that focuses on linguistic resources;
- examines how advertisements make use of language(s), including Italian and the use of English as a foreign language, in order to attract attention and persuade their audience;
- familiarises readers with response mechanisms that bilinguals and multilinguals experience when exposed to advertising in different languages;
- demonstrates both qualitative and quantitative approaches to researching the intersections between language and marketing.

Advertising and Multilingual Repertoires is key reading for postgraduate students and researchers in the field of language and advertising.

Marco Santello is a lecturer in Intercultural Competence in the School of Languages, Cultures and Societies at the University of Leeds, UK.

Advertising and Multilingual Repertoires

From linguistic resources to patterns of response

Marco Santello

Routledge
Taylor & Francis Group

LONDON AND NEW YORK

First published 2016
by Routledge

2 Park Square, Milton Park, Abingdon, Oxfordshire OX14 4RN
52 Vanderbilt Avenue, New York, NY 10017

Routledge is an imprint of the Taylor & Francis Group, an informa business

First issued in paperback 2020

British Library Cataloguing-in-Publication Data
A catalogue record for this book is available from the British Library

Library of Congress Cataloging-in-Publication Data
A catalog record for this title has been requested

ISBN: 978-1-138-21825-3 (hbk)
ISBN: 978-0-367-60748-7 (pbk)

Typeset in Times New Roman
by Apex CoVantage, LLC

Contents

Figures

Tables

Acknowledgements

I would like to express my deepest gratitude to the colleagues, family and friends who encouraged me to pursue this research and made themselves available to go through previous drafts of the book. I must also thank in particular Fabrizio Bianchi for his advice on graphs and tables and Cécile de Cat for her suggestions in the final stages of the volume. I am also extremely grateful for the assistance provided by Routledge and for the generous financial and logistic support of the University of Sydney. I have received a great amount of help from the Italian community in Australia since I started my fieldwork. I wish to gratefully acknowledge all the participants who graciously gave their time to contribute to this research. My heartfelt thanks go to my parents for their wisdom, love and for raising me bilingually.

Introduction

The centrality of the exchange of funds and goods in contemporary societies and the importance of the persuasive practices that make these exchanges possible are both widely acknowledged. This acknowledgement is at the basis of the ever-increasing interest in the functioning of language in the marketplace and, especially in the past few decades, in how advertising harnesses the power of linguistic tools to achieve its goals. However, the role that multilingual resources play in persuasion is still largely unclear, especially when these resources are meant to reach multilingual audiences. This chapter will briefly discuss the relationship between language and the market, paying particular attention to what occurs in advertising that targets multilinguals, before presenting the topic and an outline of the book.

Linguistic resources, persuasion and the market

We have long known that the ability to use linguistic resources is strongly linked with the convincing power of messages. As early as the 1st century AD, the rhetorician Quintilian (*Institutio Oratoria*, 1–24) put the mastery of linguistic skills at the centre of his suggestions on how to become a good persuader. Similarly Cicero (*De oratore*, 4–6), following Aristotle, described one's ability to construct texts through linguistic skilfulness as the central node to effective persuasion. Over the centuries intellectuals have further developed these ideas, working toward a progressive acknowledgement of the central role played by those who are reached by persuasion, and specifically their ability to recognise linguistic strategies in messages (Greimas and Courtés 1982), thereby establishing firmer links between linguistics and protreptics.

In more recent times different research traditions have tried to tease out the connections between language and advertising, making apparent that the meaning of advertising is created between the senders of an advertisement, the receivers and the texts themselves. In a keynote lecture at the 9th International Symposium on Bilingualism in 2013, the linguist Lionel Wee poignantly affirmed that various kinds of organisations employ multilingualism to interact with their clientele, instantiating the presence of an array of multilingual practices involving advertising. Wee's observations are in line with the increasing number of studies on multilingualism in advertising in recent years, where researchers have focused on how multiple languages are employed to address different audiences across a variety of contexts. Not unexpectedly the use of English alongside other languages has been shown to be one of the key 'orienting' (Blommaert 2010: 144) factors in marketing communication in a large number of arenas. As a consequence, the analysis of advertising texts that use English has been prolific and has repeatedly led to the conclusion that the choice of this language together with – or instead of – other languages intersects several characteristics of the target audience. On a similar note, in the 'site of language contact' (Piller 2003: 170) offered by marketing communication, research has identified the development of hybrid and transnational identities, shedding light on the range of features that distinguish contemporary consumers (cf. Bhatia 2000; Li 2010).

The central role of recipients is becoming increasingly clear in contemporary globalised societies where audiences and consumers experience heightened levels of participation across media. Notwithstanding this, research on how advertising and multilingualism are intertwined has not taken enough into account the processes at play when advertisers use the languages that their audiences speak, even though different audiences' repertoires have long been described as central to the construction of meaning in advertising (Eco 1987). It is especially difficult to find studies that provide data-driven examples on how to study attitudinal and response patterns of multilingual communities that are reached by campaigns that make use of their languages. Yet, we know that when the target of advertising comprises large communities of multilinguals, marketers are likely to take into account their linguistic repertoire when designing advertisements (de Bres 2014). In this way they may consider multilinguals as a subsegment of their audience, assuming that their multilingualism would impinge on their reaction to persuasive communication. In particular, since multilinguals tend to respond differently to messages conveyed in each of their languages (Luna 2011; Peracchio, Bublitz and Luna 2014; Santello 2015), choosing a language in light of specific patterns of response can be decisive in the success of an advertising campaign that addresses such an audience. As multilingual recipients of advertising, we may or may not be aware that we are classified as (potential) consumers according to the languages we know and use. Still, our multilingualism is one of the elements that impacts on the way in which we react to advertisements that employ our languages.

About this book

This monograph aims at tackling these issues by exploring the interconnections between advertising and multilingualism from a perspective that bridges applied linguistics and marketing communication research. It investigates the ways in which speakers of more than one language – in this sense, this volume refers to multilinguals including also bilinguals – relate to advertisements that use their linguistic repertoire. In particular, by focusing on Italian English speakers in Australia, the study shows that, in relation to a number of linguistic elements and marketing goals, multilinguals develop attitudes and responses to advertisements that, while generally having little or nothing to do with multilingual existence (Kelly-Holmes 2005: 173), are in fact contingent on their lived experience with the languages. The volume actively harnesses the theoretical and methodological advancements of different strands of research, taking particular care in combining the elicitation of attitudinal data through interviews with experimental data. In this way it is possible to appreciate the complexity of the relationship between speakers and languages in context, while also identifying individual variables that are responsible for specific response patterns.

This volume attempts to put front and centre the dialectic that exists between structural forces that govern the construction of texts in the backdrop of – and often in constitutive opposition to – everyday multilingualism and the circular movements that connect linguistic resources at the source and at the final end of advertising communication (Fairclough 1989: 39). Marketing scholars have already started to incorporate some advancements proposed by applied linguistics research on the relationship between commodification and texts (Hornikx and van Meurs 2015), and the ground is fertile for applied linguists to reciprocate. This would need a collective effort, but the present research tries to get a handle on the complications of interdisciplinary work by discussing the main findings of major research strands, their possible compatibility and what aggregating different perspectives can enable us to see. In doing this, this volume gives prominence to the multilingual repertoires of audiences as well as the specific goals that advertising aims to reach, unearthing surprising tensions between linguistic resources and response to persuasive messages. This examination thus aims to provide an opportunity to discern some useful elements of the little-known intersections between textual strategies that use different linguistic codes in advertising and their projected reception. These will invite us to think about the usefulness as well as the criticalities of including different sources of data when attempting to chart the terrain where the languages of advertising come to life, and will help to interrogate the possible future directions that future research might take.

Outline of the book

After this introduction, Chapter 1 presents the light under which this book inspects advertising and linguistic repertoires. It illustrates that the processes that advertising is imbued in when it interacts with multilingualism are steeped in the simplifying trends that ultimately exploit languages for commercial purposes. It will highlight some of the most important interpretative keys one can use to decipher multilingual advertising and how these point toward symbolic and socio-psychological features that generate meaning in discourse. At the same time, it will be clear that numerous scholars have implied that advertising does what it aims to do because in some ways it relates to the linguistic make-up of its intended audiences and that the role and status that languages hold among speakers is key to effective communication.

Chapter 2 delves deeper into the relationship between repertoires of actual speakers and language use in advertising. Through a discussion around some of the most recent advancements in studies on advertising to multilinguals, a number of response mechanisms will be explained, together with their predictive power and limitations. One central theme will be the mixing of languages in advertising and, specifically, in what sense codeswitching can be an effective strategy as a communicative practice that relates closely with language use in real-life contexts. It will also be clear that the fact that languages are alive within a social arena is pivotal for advertising to multilinguals, as both repertoires and socio-psychological features of languages are formed in localised environments. The chapter then provides the background from where this study starts to investigate advertising and multilingual repertoires using a broad spectrum of methods that pay special attention to the goals of advertising.

Chapter 3 shows how, thanks to an approach that places lived experiences of multilingualism at the centre, it is possible to obtain a picture of advertising and multilingualism that accounts for the relationship between repertoires and messages. Multilinguals shape their attitudes to the use of various codes in advertising building upon their direct linguistic encounters and being fully cognisant of the host of goals that advertising sets out to achieve. It is the experiential foundation of their positioning that allows attitudes to emerge in interaction within a group of speakers.

Experimental approaches that complement other methodological choices are the core of Chapter 4. It will be explained what kind of data this method can gather and the varieties of issues that one may want to pay attention to when designing studies on multilinguals. It will be apparent that, while general patterns can be broadly traced among a specific group of multilinguals, more fine-grained understanding is to be achieved through the consideration of indicators of response that go beyond evaluation. This gives room to the establishment of firmer connections between commercial objectives and the functioning of language.

Chapter 5 sheds light on what may lie behind patterns of response, and it links them explicitly to the relationship between speakers and their languages. It will be noted that the findings of some pioneering studies on advertising to multilingual audiences and the processes unveiled by discourse scholars are generally in line with the role of language attitudes in response to advertising. Furthermore, direct links between linguistic resources and patterns of response are ascertained clearly by dissecting the composition of language attitudes and matching it with specific features of the audiences' repertoires. The chapter maintains that the persuasive power of languages can be traced in the evaluative elements that connect speakers with their multilingualism.

The concluding chapter synopsises the findings and discusses the ways in which an approach that connects linguistic resources and patterns of response at various levels can be productive. The accent will be on the role of multilingual audiences and the localised nature of their response to linguistic strategies in advertising. It will be shown how this line of inquiry is in consonance with other approaches and opens spaces for further interdisciplinary endeavours, as well as offering hints for professional practice.

References

Bhatia, Tej K. 2000. *Advertising in Rural India: Language, Marketing Communication, and Consumerism.* Tokyo: Tokyo Univeristy of Foreign Studies.
Blommaert, Jan. 2010. *The Sociolinguistics of Globalization.* Cambridge; New York: Cambridge University Press.

Cicero. *De Oratore*. Ed. Jeffrey Henderson (2014). Cambridge: Harvard University Press.

de Bres, Julia. 2014. Multilingual Advertising and Regionalisation in Luxembourg. In Christian Wille, et al. (eds.) *Räume Und Identitäten in Grenzregionen. Politiken – Medien – Subjekt*. Bielefeld: Transcript. 143–56.

Eco, Umberto. 1987. Il Messaggio Pubblicitario. In Maria Luisa Altieri Biagi and Massimo Baldini (eds.) *Le Fantaparole: Il Linguaggio della Pubblicità*. Rome: Armando. 67–72.

Fairclough, Norman. 1989. *Language and Power*. London; New York: Longman.

Greimas, Algirdas Julien, and Joseph Courtés. 1982. *Semiotics and Language: An Analytical Dictionary*. Bloomington: Indiana University Press.

Hornikx, Jos, and Frank van Meurs. 2015. Foreign Language Display in Advertising from a Psycholinguistic and Sociolinguistic Perspective. In Juan Miguel Alcantara-Pilar, et al. (eds.) *Analyzing the Cultural Diversity of Consumers in the Global Marketplace*. Hershey, PA: IGI Global. 299–319.

Kelly-Holmes, Helen. 2005. *Advertising as Multilingual Communication*. Houndmills, Basingstoke, Hampshire: Palgrave Macmillan.

Li, Songqing. 2010. The Discursive Construction of Identity in Chinese-English Bilingual Advertising: A Critical Inquiry. PhD Thesis. Singapore: National University of Singapore.

Luna, David. 2011. Advertising to the Buy-Lingual Consumer. In Vivian Cook and Benedetta Bassetti (eds.) *Language and Bilingual Cognition*. Hove: Psychology. 543–58.

Peracchio, Laura, Melissa Bublitz, and David Luna. 2014. Cultural Diversity and Marketing: The Multicultural Consumer. In Verónica Benet-Martínez and Ying-yi Hong (eds.) *The Oxford Handbook of Multicultural Identity*. Oxford: Oxford University Press. 438–61.

Piller, Ingrid. 2003. Advertising as a Site of Language Contact. *Annual Review of Applied Linguistics* 23: 170–83.

Quintilian. *Institutio Oratoria*. Ed. Harold Hedgeworth Butler (1920). Cambridge: Harvard University Press.

Santello, Marco. 2015. Advertising to Italian English Bilinguals in Australia: Attitudes and Response to Language Selection. *Applied Linguistics* 36: 95–120.

1 Constructing advertising directed at multilingual audiences

1.1 Impersonal bilingualism and imitation varieties in advertising

Advertising is a form of communication that exploits a vast array of tools spanning from figures of speech to intertextuality in a way that is meant to generate a set of desired outcomes on target audiences (Myers 1994). Because of the centrality of language, it is common practice for advertising agencies to hire copywriters who can master language at an excellent level and, as a result, it is not easy to find professional copywriters who have learnt later in life the language with which they work on a daily basis (Smith and Klein-Braley 1997). For instance, while art directors in Milan can often be professionals who have moved to Italy as adults, copywriters are by and large born and raised in Italy and often also hold degrees from local universities. While this common practice is very informative on the role of language competence in the production of effective campaigns, it also reveals a hidden monolingual bias; it assumes not only the prevalence of a discourse around the supremacy of native speakerness (whatever that means) but also implicitly accepts the assumption that advertising uses only one language (cf. Dimofte, Forehand and Deshpande 2003).

On the contrary, scholars have long argued that advertising should be intended as multilingual communication, not only because it often uses a range of languages side by side in a campaign or because it mixes languages in single messages but also by virtue of the fact that varieties dialogue with each other, and through that dialogue they are transformed and consequently generate meaning (Kelly-Holmes 2005: 20–22). In contemporary globalised societies linguistic systems are not confined within national borders nor are they immobile. They circulate and become resources available for communication so that advertising has at its disposal a set of linguistic instruments that capitalise on the mobility of languages in order to achieve marketing purposes.

One can argue that the purposes of advertising would be unattainable should the language used in advertising be unrelated to the life of the audiences it reaches. In other words, it would be by virtue of the interplay between the language used in messages and the language of the audience that advertising does what it aims to do. While this argument appears unproblematic at first sight, numerous scholars have shown that advertising actually uses languages that do not necessarily belong to the repertoire of its audience.

The earliest systematic study focusing on the use of multiple languages in advertising was carried out only in relatively recent times by Haarmann (1989). In trying to identify the processes at the basis of the use of languages other than Japanese in commercials broadcast in mainstream television, he found that languages implicate cultural associations, which he called ethnocultural stereotypes. Instead of being used to convey information effectively, languages such as French and English stand for foreign cultures, which, in turn, are associated with a set of attributes. French, for instance, reminds the audience of charm, attraction, elegance and good taste (cf. also Tanaka 1999: 55–58). In addition, certain products would fit some stereotypes more than others. Hence English is more likely to be used to advertise products like sportswear, televisions and scooters, while French would be more suitable for furniture, makeup and fashion (Haarmann 1989: 99–116).

Haarmann also conducted a number of surveys that, although now outdated, reveal some interesting data on recipients as well. It seems that his respondents – young television viewers – would prefer foreign languages especially when they are used for luxury products such as good-quality cosmetics and cars. Predictably, these specifications vary a great deal across different markets. Haarmann delineates similarities and differences between the situation in Japan and what happens, for example, in Malta and in some Scandinavian countries. In keeping with this, some other scholars have highlighted that, for instance, the French language in non-francophone countries would bring to mind a network of associations such as refined taste and sophistication, which can be exploited in marketing communications in order to increase positive attitudes toward brands (Leclerc, Schmitt and Dubé 1994: 269–70).

Following these findings Haarmann developed the useful concept of impersonal multilingualism. He observed that the most widespread language in

Japanese advertising (alongside the national language) by far is English, although the language has a minor role in the multilingualism of the country (Noguchi and Fotos 2001: 329), while other languages hold a more prominent role (Cary 2001: 98–132). Moreover, although English is taught extensively in the country, not many Japanese are able to hold a full conversation using the language. This contrast between the real language permeation in the country and its exposure in advertising is the reason why this form of multilingualism is called impersonal. As opposed to societal multilingualism, impersonal multilingualism cannot be experienced in everyday personal communication, but it is solely rooted in the mediascape. In other words, the choice of English in Japanese advertising has nothing to do with the real diffusion of the language among people and thus exemplifies an exclusive media-specific type of usage. According to this view the fact that the languages used in advertising do not belong to the repertoire of the audience is one key factor that contributes to their success as instruments of persuasion.

The ethnocultural stereotypes at the basis of the impersonal multilingualism of advertising have numerous possible combinations and are liable to fluctuate according to different contexts (cf. Myers 1994: 92–96), but they all serve some distinctive purposes connected to 'ethnosymbolism' (Haarmann 1986: 109). These purposes are described by Bhatia and Ritchie (2006) as being linked to socio-psychological elements. In their view socio-psychological elements of languages are the features of languages that can be exploited to produce meaning in advertising. Rather similar to the symbolic functions, socio-psychological elements can be identified in numerous forms in a wide variety of environments, specifically in relation to the English language. As I will discuss later, these socio-psychological features are involved in the processes of construction of multilingual texts in that they serve as tools to enhance the creativity that advertising is based upon. Moreover, these features capitalise on the associations with multilingualism that audiences hold in relation to advertising, thus reaching the desired intents.

Notions to those developed by Haarmann, Bhatia and Ritchie have also been developed by Kelly-Holmes (2005), who reaffirms that, although multilingualism in advertising may have both informative and symbolic functions, the latter is much more likely than the former. According to her analysis conducted in Ireland but also considering advertising from other countries, the nature of multiple language use in advertising directed at the general audience is chiefly symbolic (cf. also Kinder 2009; Declercq 2011). In other words, there is no communicative or utility value in using more languages in this context, or it has been obscured to the point of becoming irrelevant. The true significance of using a foreign language is connected to the aim of selling a country of origin or, better, the image of a country. Associating a country to a brand helps to communicate a wide range of attributes, none of which has informative denotations; instead they are all linked to stereotypes that originate in the intrinsic reductivism of this 'fake multilingualism' (*ibid*: 185). The main associations with the English language – e.g. modernity, internationalism, cosmopolitarianism, trendiness, success – are the exemplification of gross, commercially driven generalisations, of which Kelly-Holmes has a fairly negative view.

In her perspective, indeed, multilingualism in advertising is a fetish in the Marxian meaning of the term. Multilingualism is charged with symbolic attributions which serve the market by attracting consumers to the object of desire; it is fundamentally ethnocentric and exploits languages for their exchange value. In other words, language in this environment creates in-groups and out-groups associated with different features, somehow akin to what happens in linguistic landscapes (cf. Sebba 2011: 457). The brands, symbolically enhanced by foreign languages, would then lead the audience to feel the desire to own some of the features belonging to the out-group. The stereotyped concepts of 'foreignness' or otherness in the country-of-origin market discourse are supported by a linguistic fetish which has more to do with fiction than reality. In this sense language is used "to refer or identify with a group, not the group being addressed, [. . .] but the group being referred to" (Kelly-Holmes 2005: 13).

A very interesting interpretative key singled out by Kelly-Holmes is the application in advertising of the notion of heteroglossia introduced for the first time by the Russian philosopher Mikhail Bakhtin (1981/1934) with regard to the polyphonic nature of literary language. Heteroglossia is the coexistence of different varieties within a single linguistic code and refers to the idea that varieties dialogue with each other, and through that dialogue they are transformed (Kelly-Holmes 2005: 20–22). As mentioned previously with regard to multilingual advertising, along this process not only do borrowed words gain new connotations but also borrowing languages mutate. Overall, therefore, multilingualism in advertising can go far beyond a sheer juxtaposition of languages and may be able to enhance meaning through internal processes of change. These processes of change are also apparent when foreign languages are used in their 'imitation varieties' (Martin 2005: 33–38). That is, the symbolic function of foreign languages may be so important that advertisers can decide to modulate the language in such a way that it becomes extremely suggestive but may end up being unintelligible. The variety employed then becomes an imitation or a resemblance of the original language and "it is simply inserted to create a certain atmosphere" (*ibid*: 36).

1.2 Choosing a language, relating to audiences

Numerous researchers have therefore made clear that languages in advertising are tools that are not meant to be instruments to convey information but rather are used as symbolic enhancers. Because of this they would not need to match the repertoire of the audience. What is more, it seems that it is by virtue of the difference between the repertoire of the audience and the codes put in place by advertising that the construction of texts works well.

These assumptions capture the common practice whereby advertising, as opposed to simply using languages as codes to communicate, exploits them disregarding their cultural depth and turning them into marketing tools. These marketing tools embody a form of multilingualism that necessarily differs from the one experienced in society, simply because it serves different purposes (Sebba 2012). However, for any code to be effective, it needs to relate in some way with its audience. Even when the content of the message is partly lost because the audience cannot make sense of it, it still speaks to a set of linguistic resources that belong to the repertoire of the audience. In this sense the multilingualism of the audience is always engaged in a dialogue with the language(s) used in a message, both when it matches it in some ways and when it does not (Bhatia 2000: 124–25). It is the case of the use of English in many parts of the world; choosing English as a code that serves the aims of advertising necessarily resonate in various ways with the linguistic resources of the audience.

English in advertising, as it is the 'hypercentral language' (Kelly-Holmes 2006: 514) holding a hegemonic position in advertising throughout the world (Frith and Mueller 2007: 33), is never considered a minority language no matter what advertising context it is used in. It may be used as a 'lingua franca' (Martin 2005: 37), a 'cool language' (Kelly-Holmes 2005: 73–75), or as a tool to render advertising international (Myers 1999: 64–67). In any case, it seems to be effective in most of the countries in which its use has been studied, in spite of the strong differences from one context to the other, precisely because it relates – if not belongs – to the repertoires of the audiences.

In Switzerland the presence of English in advertising affords Swiss audiences the feeling of possessing some attributes, such as professional appeal, associated with English but not with the national languages (Cheshire and Moser 1994). In Russia, Western culture, through the use of English, is represented in TV commercials, which seem to influence the values and the beliefs that advertising communicates (Ustinova 2003). In the same context English also serves purposes connected to psychological reasons, i.e. attracting attention, and functional reasons (Ustinova and Bhatia 2005). Further, individualism, high self-esteem, success in the public arena and fun in life are identified as core cultural values encoded in advertising and, through language choice, communicated to audiences (Ustinova 2006).

By examining advertising across six cultures, Bhatia (1992) shows that the use of English involves processes that go beyond the exploitation of its symbolic features. In his view, one noteworthy and somewhat underestimated purpose resides in the phonological and syntactic adaptations that English allows. Under this perspective, English can be seen as one of the many creative tools that copywriters utilise to produce the desired effect of persuasion. The linguistic innovations, adaptations and loan translations common in the global use of English seem to be greatly expressed in advertising, probably due to the creative needs of this particular kind of communication. Moreover, Bhatia suggests that the use of English stimulates syntactic violations and ungrammaticality that are able to achieve creative effects, thanks indeed to the possibility of bending the limits of grammar that English affords advertisers.

A recent article, however, interestingly discusses some features of English in advertising that go beyond the range of positive connotations normally associated with the language (Kuppens 2010). It argues that the use of a specific foreign language taps into the possible intertextual references that the audience can tie to advertising. For example, British English can serve as an instrument to support an advertisement that resembles wildlife documentaries. Likewise, American English can relate to dialogic sports commentary and syrupy Hollywood drama. In these situations English may be even mocked or parodied, thus subverting the usual conventions of its linguistic superiority. It therefore relates deeply to the repertoires of the audiences: it is thanks to the use of one language in relation to a specific message that texts are constructed in opposition or in consonance with assumed linguistic norms spread among audiences.

1.3 Mixing languages

Choosing a language to build persuasive communication is not the only strategy that advertisers can implement. Numerous researchers have pointed out that mixing languages within one single advertisement is common and perhaps even prevalent in contemporary advertising. In analysis of language mixing in France, for instance, Martin (2002: 385–99) notes that the specific mix of English and French in texts can determine successful results. Although some consumers may consider the use of English in France a threat to the cultural and linguistic identity of the country (Frith and Mueller 2007: 33), it seems that foreign languages represent the 'glocal' linguistic and cultural reality of the French market (Martin 2007: 187). In other words, not only is the selection of a language an important instrument for the construction of texts but the mix of languages holds paramount importance. In fact, language choice is only one tool that can be employed to reach audiences; a very common tactic is to avoid a univocal language choice and opt for a multilingual construction of texts. This kind of choice is also normal in rural India, where the mix of languages and scripts overcomes the dichotomy between English and Indian languages that permeates media and advertising discourse against the backdrop of a highly multilingual country (Bhatia 2000: 154–65).

Further demonstrating the importance of language mixing in advertising, Bhatia and Ritchie (2006) have analysed the use of English not in isolation but alongside other languages in several countries belonging to the so-called outer and expanding circles. They conclude that English has undergone a process of 'glocalisation' – concurrent globalisation and localisation – and that this is to be linked to the demand of creativity that ultimately promotes multilingualism worldwide. Moreover, they have highlighted that different parts of advertising messages, called structural domains, are more likely to lead to English being inserted in the text. Several forms of insertion of English constitute a variety of communicative efforts, all of which account for the significance of language mixing in advertising texts.

Something comparable emerges from a study in Germany (Piller 2001). About seventy per cent of more than four hundred print advertisements in Piller's corpus showed some form of ethnosymbolism associated with the concurrent use of a number of languages. Moreover, the author underscores the main features of what she calls 'the implied reader', which may be defined as the addressee or target. It is an international consumer that is characterised by "internationalism, future orientation, success and elitism, as well as youth and proclivity to enjoy the good things in life" (*ibid*: 180) and, one could add, knowledge of more than one language.

A study conducted in China by Li (2010) also shows that multilingualism in advertising can contribute to the shaping of social identities and that advertisers do not use undifferentiated global languages and apply them to advertisements simply in order to exploit their connotations. Rather, advertisers tend to selectively appropriate social styles of languages, turning them into a local practice. In this way, languages acquire a focal role in the construction of global identities involving the simultaneous articulation of contrary elements that are typical of the modern hybrid and multiple identities of Chinese audiences. Specifically, the collective identities of gender, nation, class and race are being affected by the usage of English in advertising thanks to its multidimensionality and its characteristics that may "vary between being decisive and being complementary, marginal or sometimes conflicting" (*ibid*: 272).

In Brazil "local creativity can do better with the availability of more than one code, of more than Portuguese alone" (Friedrich 2002: 28). In that context, too, the properties of another language, such as length of words, are believed to provide extra linguistic material that can be used in combination with other codes by those who create advertising. The same happens in Southern India, where "the use of English in Tamil media enlarges and exploits the available stylistic range, and makes the language appealing" (Krishnasamy 2007: 47). In other words, not only does English offer the possibility of breaking grammatical rules that would be problematic in some other linguistic systems, but multilingualism itself allows innovations and an enhanced degree of creativity.

Likewise, the use of both English and Indian languages "has become a common advertising strategy in India" (Gupta 2007: 11). English words in Indian advertising are also described as conveying a "modern or cosmopolitan image of the product or the company" (*ibid*: 3) and as being indispensible for creativity (Kathpalia and Ong 2015). According to Serra (2006), in Italy the usage of multilingualism is not only an instrument to capture the audience's attention and to afford relevance to particular parts of advertisements, but also a way to incorporate some general connotations that languages carry. Similarly, Takashi (1991) carried out an extensive and rigorous functional analysis of Japanese advertising to verify the relationship between several variables (e.g. written versus spoken language modality, audience characteristics, product types, etc.) and loanwords in advertising (cf. also Sherry and Camargo 1987).

In her analysis of TV advertising in New Zealand, de Bres (2010) acutely observes that languages in advertising are deeply intertwined with the knowledge audiences have of the languages employed. Moreover, the role and status these languages hold among speakers and non-speakers have an impact on the ways in which advertising plans to obtain its desired outcomes.

The use of more than one language in single advertisements implies a set of audiences that are characterised by various degrees of language competence and that, by virtue of that competence and the status of their languages in society, can relate to the messages.

1.4 Beyond intended audiences

One central matter that studies on the interactions between multilingualism and advertising have recurrently unpicked is the fracture between societal language use and language use in the mediascape, poignantly encapsulated by the notion of impersonal bilingualism. Its being linked with the exploitation of language for commercial purposes seems to be intrinsic to advertising communication; one can barely find any examples in the literature where multilingualism is handled by advertisers beyond such exploitation. In this sense languages are even meant to be fetishised through advertising, while at the same time participating in multilayered identity work that is creatively achieved at the interfaces of global and local sites. Further, the construction of advertising is to be understood precisely in light of the range of tools that allow the re-articulation of multilingualism in the commercial sphere. Advertising texts use a variety of linguistic strategies that involve the choice of a code and their possible mix with others, thereby creating an interaction with perspective audiences and their pre-existing linguistic knowledge. Thus multilingual advertising, despite establishing forms of impersonal bilingualism and language fetish, in actual fact speaks to societal multilingualism, as implied by both Bhatia (2000; 2001) and Kelly-Holmes (2005; 2006) and more recently by Kathpalia and Ong (2015).

In the following chapters I will argue that, by keeping these processes in sight, one can comprehend advertising in multilingual contexts. As a prompting read, perhaps it is worth taking a look back at the authoritative volume written by Guy Cook on the discourse of advertising, which condenses some striking features of the discourse-related approach dominating the subfield. In the section dedicated to the 'people' (Cook 2001: 171–237), the author relies strongly on textual analysis, where analogies between literature and advertising are pointed out as tools to understand advertising discourse. Furthermore, when dealing with the reception of advertising, he refers to artists, writers and academics. From 2001 many steps have been taken to integrate Cook's approach to language in advertising, but in many ways there is still a long way to go if we really want to come to grips with the interaction between messages and multilingual audiences. The next chapters discuss how multilinguals process and respond to linguistic strategies and what response mechanisms underpin the interaction between texts and their recipients.

References

Bakhtin, Mikhail M. 1981/1934. Discourse in the Novel. In Michael Holquist (ed.) *The Dialogic Imagination*. Austin: University of Texas Press. 259–422.

Bhatia, Tej K. 1992. Discourse Functions and Pragmatics of Mixing: Advertising across Cultures. *World Englishes* 11: 195–215.

Bhatia, Tej K. 2000. *Advertising in Rural India: Language, Marketing Communication, and Consumerism*. Tokyo: Tokyo Univeristy of Foreign Studies.

Bhatia, Tej K. 2001. Language Mixing in Global Advertising. In Edwin Thumboo (ed.) *The Three Circles of English*. Singapore: Singapore University Press. 195–215.

Bhatia, Tej K., and William C. Ritchie. 2006. Bilingualism in the Global Media and Advertising. In Tej K. Bhatia and William C. Ritchie (eds.) *The Handbook of Bilingualism*. Malden, MA: Blackwell Publishing. 513–16.

Cary, Ann B. 2001. Affiliation, Not Assimilation: Resident Koreans and Ethnic Education. In Mary Goebel Noguchi and Sandra Fotos (eds.) *Studies in Japanese Bilingualism*. Clevedon: Multilingual Matters.

Cheshire, Jenny, and Lise-Marie Moser. 1994. English as a Cultural Symbol: The Case of Advertisements in French-Speaking Switzerland. *Journal of Multilingual and Multicultural Development* 15: 451–69.

Cook, Guy. 2001. *The Discourse of Advertising*. London: Routledge.

de Bres, Julia. 2010. Promoting a Minority Language to Majority Language Speakers: Television Advertising about the Māori Language Targeting Non-Māori New Zealanders. *Journal of Multilingual and Multicultural Development* 31: 515–29.

Declercq, Christophe. 2011. Advertising and Localization. In Kirsten Malmkjær and Kevin Windle (eds.) *The Oxford Handbook of Translation Studies*. Oxford; New York: Oxford University Press. 262–74.

Dimofte, Claudiu V., Mark R. Forehand, and Rohit Deshpande. 2003. Ad Schema Incongruity as Elicitor of Ethnic Self-Awareness and Differential Advertising Response. *Journal of Advertising* 32: 7–17.

Friedrich, Patricia. 2002. English in Advertising and Brand Naming: Sociolinguistic Considerations and the Case of Brazil. *English Today* 18: 21–28.

Frith, Katherine Torland, and Barbara Mueller. 2007. *Advertising and Societies: Global Issues*. New York: Peter Lang.

Gupta, Renu. 2007. Bilingual Advertising in a Multilingual Country. *Language in India* 7: 8–9.

Haarmann, Harald. 1986. Verbal Strategies in Japanese Fashion Magazines: A Study in Impersonal Bilingualism and Ethnosymbolism. *International Journal of the Sociology of Language* 58: 107–21.

Haarmann, Harald. 1989. *Symbolic Values of Foreign Language Use*. Berlin: Mouton de Gruyter.

Kathpalia, Sujata Surinder, and Kenneth Keng Wee Ong. 2015. The Use of Code-Mixing in Indian Billboard Advertising. *World Englishes* 34: 557–575.

Kelly-Holmes, Helen. 2005. *Advertising as Multilingual Communication*. Houndmills, Basingstoke, Hampshire: Palgrave Macmillan.

Kelly-Holmes, Helen. 2006. Multilingualism and Commercial Language Practices on the Internet. *Journal of Sociolinguistics* 10: 507–19.

Kinder, John J. 2009. Immigration, Integration and Dialects: Reflections on a Recent Italian Government Advertising Campaign. *Fulgor* 4: 12–27.

Krishnasamy, Kanthimathi. 2007. English in Tamil: The Language of Advertising. *English Today* 23: 40–49.

Kuppens, An H. 2010. English in Advertising: Generic Intertextuality in a Globalizing Media Environment. *Applied Linguistics* 31: 115–35.

Leclerc, France, Bernd H. Schmitt, and Laurette Dubé. 1994. Foreign Branding and Its Effects on Product Perceptions and Attitudes. *Journal of Marketing Research* 31: 263–70.

Li, Songqing. 2010. The Discursive Construction of Identity in Chinese-English Bilingual Advertising: A Critical Inquiry. PhD Thesis. Singapore: National University of Singapore.

Martin, Elizabeth. 2002. Mixing English in French Advertising. *World Englishes* 21: 375–402.

Martin, Elizabeth. 2005. *Marketing Identities through Language: English and Global Imagery in French Advertising*. Basingstoke: Palgrave Macmillan.

Martin, Elizabeth. 2007. 'Frenglish' for Sale: Multilingual Discourses for Addressing Today's Global Consumer. *World Englishes* 26: 170–88.

Myers, Greg. 1994. *Words in Ads*. London: Arnold.

Myers, Greg. 1999. *Ad Worlds: Brands, Media, Audiences*. London: Arnold.

Noguchi, Mary Goebel, and Sandra Fotos. 2001. *Studies in Japanese Bilingualism*. Clavedon: Multilingual Matters.

Piller, Ingrid. 2001. Identity Constructions in Multilingual Advertising. *Language in Society* 30: 153–86.

Sebba, Mark. 2011. Societal Bilingualism. In Barbara Johnstone, Ruth Wodak and Paul Kerswill (eds.) *The Sage Handbook of Sociolinguistics*. Los Angeles: Sage. 445–59.

Sebba, Mark. 2012. Researching and Theorising Multilingual Texts. In Mark Sebba, Shahrzad Mahootian and Carla Jonsson (eds.) *Language Mixing and Code-Switching in Writing: Approaches to Mixed-Language Written Discourse*. New York: Routledge. 1–26.

Serra, Alessandra. 2006. *L'uso Dell'inglese Nella Pubblicità Italiana*. Rome: Aracne.

Sherry, John F. Jr., and Eduardo G. Camargo. 1987. "May Your Life Be Marvelous": English Language Labelling and the Semiotics of Japanese Promotion. *Journal of Consumer Research* 14: 174–88.

Smith, Veronica, and Christine Klein-Braley. 1997. Advertising – a Five Stage Strategy for Translation. In M. Snell-Hornby, Z. Jettmarova and K. Kaindl (eds.) *Translation as Intercultural Communication*. Amsterdam: John Benjamins. 173–84.

Takashi, Kyoko. 1991. A Functional Analysis of English Borrowings in Japanese Advertising: Linguistics and Sociolinguistic Perspectives. PhD Thesis. Washington, DC: Georgetown University.

Tanaka, Keiko. 1999. *Advertising Language: A Pragmatic Approach to Advertisements in Britain and Japan.* London: Routledge.

Ustinova, Irina P. 2003. Impact of English on Modern Russian TV Advertising. PhD Thesis. Syracuse, NY: Syracuse University.

Ustinova, Irina P. 2006. English and Emerging Advertising in Russia. *World Englishes* 25: 267–77.

Ustinova, Irina P., and Tej K. Bhatia. 2005. Convergence of English in Russian TV Commercials. *World Englishes* 24: 495–508.

2 Language effects on multilingual speakers

2.1 Approaching response and determining effective ways to target multilinguals

If the linguistic tools that advertisers employ are related to the repertoires of their intended audience, then turning our attention to what happens when audiences decode messages is a productive endeavour. Traditionally scholars have tried to understand the work of advertising in all its components by analysing texts and inferring audiences from their construction as perspective target (Hmensa 2010). Evidently this inference is useful insofar as it accounts for the processes that happen at a discursive level but leaves the response of the audience outside the principal focus of research. Bullo (2014) discusses this problem, highlighting that discursive researchers, who constitute the large majority of the linguists working on advertising, see social representations as originating from discursive practices. This approach is in many ways awaiting complementation in that the role of cognition still needs to be explored in conjunction with textual components (*ibid*: 36). In other words, not only the context of production but also the context of reception needs to be analysed.

This lacuna has been implied in a large body of previous research. Bhatia (2000: 291), for instance, has clearly stated that the success of an advertisement lies in its ability to relate to consumers, and de Bres (2010) has linked it directly with the use of different languages. Nevertheless, it is thanks to researchers who come from marketing research traditions that we have come to know some key response mechanisms relating to the use of languages in advertising. These researchers are interested in hypothetical real-life situations where advertisers who seek to target a multilingual population can choose one of the languages that the audience understands. What

advertisers aim to do is to choose the language that will best serve their marketing goals, and they wish to know from researchers how this choice can
be made. The answer given by researchers is that one must verify that the
goals are met by eliciting response among the multilinguals that are meant
to be reached by advertising (Luna 2011). The problem is that many scholars have developed a heterogeneous set of dependent variables to assess
and explain the effectiveness of advertising, using for example perceived
sensitivity of advertisers, comprehension, recall and recognition, attitudes
toward advertisements, attitudes toward products advertised and perceived
originality. Most of these variables have been tested through multi-item
scales, which tend to vary across studies.

This high heterogeneity in terms of variables is particularly evident if we
look at the study by Koslow, Shamdasani and Touchstone (1994), which in
many ways paves the way for all subsequent studies. Their work attempts
to understand how a migrant group responds to advertisements written in its
community language. The authors take into consideration the Hispanic community in the United States and focus on the response to the use of Spanish
in advertising to that community. They argue that from a sociolinguistic
point of view, the use of Spanish in advertising targeting the Hispanic community can be viewed as a manifestation of the well-studied linguistic phenomenon called accommodation. Accommodation theory postulates that a
speaker would try to be closer to the interlocutor by choosing a language
easier for the counterpart (Giles et al. 1979; Giles, Coupland and Coupland
1991). In turn this effort is viewed positively and generates a more favourable evaluation of the speaker. In addition, the greater the effort to accom-
modate to the language of the interlocutor, the more the speaker will be
perceived as sensitive toward it. While this theory has been applied before
to mass communication (Giles, Coupland and Coupland 1991; Green 1999),
Koslow and colleagues are the first to examine its importance in advertising to multilinguals. In their study they hypothesise that an advertiser can
decide to employ a minority language to gain an image of sensitivity toward
that community, thereby obtaining appreciation from its audience, and in
order to test this hypothesis the researchers created questionnaires through
which participants were asked to rate four advertisements according to the
perceived sensitivity of the advertiser. Three independent variables were
tested. The first was language dominance, which resulted from multiple
scales including language used at home and at work, Spanish TV viewer-
ship, monolingual versus multilingual language ability[1] and first language.
The second was language attitude, resulting from perceived friendliness,

convincing ability and influence of the languages. The third was language of the advertisements, which could have been English only, Spanish only, Spanish with subtitles in English or English with subtitles in Spanish.

The hypothesis was fully supported by the outcomes of their experiments, as the participants rated more favourably advertisers who used Spanish together with English in their advertisements directed at Hispanics. However – and perhaps more interestingly – the results revealed that advertising in Spanish only diminished the effect provided by the accommodation effort, a phenomenon explained by the authors as a language-related inferiority complex. In other words, when the only language used is Spanish, the choice is no longer perceived as sensitive toward the community because an inferiority complex would be aroused. These scholars connect the result to the fact that attitude toward Spanish can be very negative in the United States, where "racism towards Hispanics is often expressed through disparaging the use of Spanish in public settings" (Koslow, Shamdasani and Touchstone 1994: 577). This would be in keeping with a certain discourse that objects to a particular language choice in advertising because of the "image of backwardness associated with that language and culture" (Grin 1994: 277).

Whether or not we agree with their conclusions, it is clear that Koslow and colleagues had already understood in 1994 that a number of factors shape the response mechanisms that multilinguals display and, most importantly, that languages are alive within social contexts that, in turn, have an impact on response. What these factors are and how response can be successfully operationalised, however, needed to be ascertained.

2.2 Choosing a language, relating to audiences and eliciting response

Luna and Peracchio (2001) were among the first to try to answer the question of why one language is more effective than another when targeting multilinguals. Their article about moderators of language effects in advertising to multilinguals argues that second-language (L2) messages result in inferior memory as compared with first-language (L1) messages. The two researchers focus on the different processing paths of L1 and L2 messages by extending the Revised Hierarchical Model (Kroll and Stewart 1994) to advertising, which describes how bilingual individuals process words corresponding to two languages. The model suggests that conceptual or semantic processing is less likely to occur when a word is encountered in an individual's second language than when it is presented in his/her first language. Thus, the RHM implies that memory for second-language messages will be inferior to memory for first-language messages (Luna and Peracchio 2001: 284).

Through a series of experiments Luna and Peracchio demonstrate that, because the conceptual links of the L2 are weaker than L1 links, L2 messages are less likely to be processed at a conceptual level and consequently cannot be stored in the mind as much as L1 stimuli. According to the researchers, in order to avoid such a negative outcome, advertisers willing to use an L2 should enhance the text-image congruity of messages, thus giving the audience the support that is able to counterbalance the superiority of the L1. Not surprisingly, congruity along with language has been proven fundamental also in the electronic marketing context and, specifically, on multilingual Internet sites (Luna, Peracchio and de Juan 2003). In addition, enhanced motivation to read and understand the advertisements has been found to impact the way multilinguals process advertising, but only when the messages are conveyed in their L1. In other words, while picture-text congruity improves the recall of both L1 and L2 messages, higher levels of motivation have a positive effect only on the processing of L1 advertisements. This is due to the fact that an inferior likelihood of conceptual processing of L2 messages blocks the potential positive effect of high motivation.

Subsequent studies (Luna and Peracchio 2002; Luna and Peracchio 2003; Wyer 2002) tend to reaffirm the general assumption that, from a cognitive perspective, the most effective language in advertising to multilinguals is the language in which the audience is more proficient, which they call *language effect*. In addition, these studies demonstrate that the need for cognition is another crucial factor in determining the way advertisements are elaborated. As readers process advertisements, their focus varies according to the perceived difficulty of the text. A challenging L2 text leads the reader to concentrate on it in order to try to decipher its content. The same is not true for challenging L1 texts, which tend to have multilinguals turn their attention toward other parts of the advertisement. Thus, the need for cognition plays an important role in the way multilinguals process advertising.[2]

Notwithstanding the robustness of the results described above, a number of studies conducted in other contexts shed light on dissimilar patterns of response. In particular, a study carried out in Malta (Caruana and Abdilla 2005) suggests that some of the findings of studies of the Hispanic community in the US cannot be generalised to all multilingual communities. Given that a great number of Maltese citizens can be considered multilingual, having Maltese as their first language and English as their second, from a psycholinguistic perspective it is expected that these multilinguals would respond more favourably to Maltese advertisements than to English ones, because of the enhanced ease of processing of messages in L1 as compared to messages in L2. However, it has been found that using Maltese instead of English in television commercials does not improve the audience's response. Although these results are confined to only one product category (cf. also Hooft and Truong 2012), and response is measured through a multidimensional scale that does not consider indicators used in previous research, this study seems to challenge the research outcomes obtained among Hispanics. In this context where a very different group of speakers is studied, response to advertising shows a different configuration, i.e. response does not favour messages in the dominant language of the audience. Therefore, even though these results cannot be directly compared to those obtained in studies conducted in the US, it is interesting to note that they tend not to confirm the findings of the studies conducted on Spanish English bilinguals of Hispanic descent.

Another set of data gathered in a non-Hispanic context concerns the comparison between the different mental processing of logographic and alphabetical languages. In a study on the different interaction of auditory and visual elements with Chinese and English (Tavassoli and Lee 2003), it has been discovered that the interference of nonverbal stimuli works differently in the two languages, such that nonverbal auditory stimuli interfere more than nonverbal visual stimuli in English, whereas the exact opposite is true for logographic Chinese. Additionally, in terms of memory, auditory cues are more effective in English and visual cues are more effective in Chinese. These results thus indicate that the language pair under study has an impact on the way multilinguals react to different languages in advertising. Using similar methods, a study conducted in Belgium among French Dutch bilinguals (Puntoni, De Langhe and Van Osselaer 2009) sheds light on an additional important aspect of language choice in advertising, i.e. the degree of emotionality carried by languages. The authors hypothesise that one's first language has a higher degree of emotionality, and therefore messages expressed in that language are likely to be perceived as more emotional than L2 messages, especially for advertising slogans. In order to test this assumption, they asked participants to rate a number of print advertisements according to a one-item seven-point scale devised to assess emotional involvement. The results of the research show that L1 messages elicit more emotional involvement and also that this phenomenon is caused neither by stereotypes nor by a difference in comprehension between the two languages. The authors propose that marketing slogans function as cues able to activate distinct memories and therefore trigger feelings experienced before in a same-language context. Hence, advertisers should take into consideration not only the audience's first language but also the language in which specific memories are stored. That is, some memories are activated more strongly by L2 messages if the situations that created those memories were experienced in an L2 context of language use. If these memories include something crucial for the goals of advertising, such as important attributes of the brand or maybe the brand name itself, then it would be a mistake to advertise in L1. Thus, apart from the general assumption that one's first language is overall more emotional than other languages, the relative differential emotionality of languages is largely connected to episodic and autobiographical memories.

In light of these results we notice that, looking back, Noriega had already highlighted similar trends in his doctoral thesis and a subsequent article (Noriega 2006; Noriega and Blair 2008). Adopting a psycholinguistic approach, he found that different languages are able to cue different thoughts. Specifically, the choice of Spanish in advertising to the Hispanic community in the US seems to evoke associations with family, friends, home and homeland; not only can single words generate different affective reactions according to the language in which they are expressed, but also the language itself can trigger some thoughts instead of others. This effect can also be moderated by the consumption context in which the advertisement is presented. The accessibility of memories and the process of thought-creation are to a great extent influenced by language choice.

These findings are consistent with the Conceptual Feature Model (Luna and Peracchio 2004), according to which words are connected to a series of concepts that determine their meaning in each individual's experience. Because one word can be learnt in a different context and associated with distinct attributes and lexical values, the set of concepts it can elicit is different across different individuals. For instance, the word 'friend' may be related to concepts such as 'honesty' and 'smile' in one individual, whereas in another it may be associated with 'toys' and 'play'. According to Luna and Peracchio, despite the broad range of possible concepts linkable to any words, some conceptual features tend to remain constant across one single language, but vary in their translation-equivalents. Thus, the word 'friend' may activate distinct conceptual features when expressed in English instead of as 'amigo' in Spanish. The researchers also show that these language-specific schemas emerge not only among monolinguals but also among multilinguals, and refer to this phenomenon as cognitive duality. They maintain that cognitive duality is the changing factor to be addressed by advertisers targeting multilinguals, in that word associations may be used appropriately to favour an advertisement through an accurate language choice.

Carroll has also explored the significance of context in the effectiveness of language choice in advertising to multilinguals (Carroll 2008; Carroll and Luna 2011), taking into consideration the theory of language domains (Fishman 1964: 37; Li 2000: 55). In an advertising context, an individual receiving a message in which the language is chosen according to language domains will experience enhanced ease of processing, and the source will benefit from that ease in terms of more positive evaluation. Thus language domains are all important for language in advertising: if the language chosen is consistent with its domains, then selecting that language will generally lead to higher evaluations. This result can be further enhanced by higher language fluency of the addressees in the chosen language. Indeed, from previous findings we know that L1 words are more accessible than L2 words and that accessibility is increased if the words are used with relative frequency. The subsequent processing fluency effect, called the 'Carroll effect' (Santello 2015: 99), brings about affective metacognitive states that, in turn, lead to better evaluations. The Carroll effect is strongly consistent with previous studies and seems to be one of the first phenomena connected specifically with the sociolinguistic complexity of multilingualism. Understanding the audience's language competence and language use is therefore crucial for the assessment of how speakers of more than one language respond to advertising.

2.3 Mixing languages and eliciting response

Understanding the linguistic reality of the multilingual speakers that advertising intends to address appears key to successful communication. Such linguistic reality we know encompasses very often various forms of language mixing as normal practice in multilinguals' daily lives (Blom and Gumperz 2000; Auer 2002; Li Wei 2005; Li Wei 2011). Should then advertisers use codeswitching to target multilinguals? Is it an effective tool to get closer to the ways in which the audiences communicate and thus be effective?

Language contact phenomena have been studied in an extremely vast array of ways by different scholars and, more generally, the definition of phenomena such as codeswitching and borrowing raises a number of issues concerning their very nature and the existence of a clear boundary between them. Rosignoli (2011: 215), for instance, proposes that flagging in codeswitched conversations tends to denote the existence of a continuum between codeswitching and borrowing. Analogously, Gardner-Chloros (2009), by using examples drawn from both written and oral texts, upholds the necessity of avoiding detrimental separations between such closely connected language phenomena. Other scholars (e.g. Poplack 1988; 2000), however, while not dismissing the existence of such a continuum between various forms of language contact phenomena, maintain the necessity to keep them separate. Further discussion of these issues is definitely beyond the scope of this brief monograph, as I deal with codeswitching, borrowing and interferences only tangentially. Suffice it here to say that I chose to adopt mainly Grosjean's terms, whereby multilinguals are defined as those who use two or more languages (or dialects) in their everyday lives (Grosjean 2010: 4), and borrowing is the inclusion of a word or expression that belongs to the less-activated language into the base or matrix language by adapting it morphologically and often phonologically (*ibid*: 58), whereas codeswitching is the alternate use of two languages where a language is used for a word, phrase or sentence while the other language remains prevalent (*ibid*: 51–52).

In the area of research on codeswitching, the specific area of codeswitching in advertising to multilinguals is at an early stage, so it is problematic to identify major findings that have found agreement among researchers. Moreover, looking at the studies that deal with this topic we notice 1) inconsistency both in choosing independent and dependent variables;[3] 2) difficulty in categorising single studies according to the approach adopted; and 3) lack of a common terminology.

One of the first attempts in this area is reported in a group of articles published between 2004 and 2005 (Luna 2004; Luna, Lerman and Peracchio 2005a; 2005b; Luna and Peracchio 2005b). While one publication focused on the grammaticality of codeswitching (Luna, Lerman and Peracchio 2005a), the bulk of research has delved into the direction of codeswitching and the variables involved in its effectiveness. For the scope of this book, I will focus on the studies dealing with direction of codeswitching as they point toward some elements of interest: language attitudes, attitudes toward codeswitching, and adherence to linguistic and media-related norms.

A groundbreaking article by Luna and Peracchio (2005b) started to explore the importance of the direction of codeswitching in evaluations of advertising. When devising a codeswitched slogan a copywriter has the power to decide whether to start with one language or the other: a slogan in an advertisement targeting a multilingual community could commence with the majority language and end with the minority language, or the reverse. It appears that minority-to-majority slogans usually work better than majority-to-minority ones. For instance, in some advertising targeting US Hispanics, slogans beginning in Spanish and finishing in English are generally viewed more positively than slogans written in the opposite direction. The authors explain this phenomenon both with cognitive salience and language attitudes. They claim that majority languages are associated with more positive concepts, such as progress, education and integration, whereas minority languages elicit marginalisation, discrimination and feelings of inferiority (Luna 2004: 150). Placing instances of the language toward which speakers have the most positive attitude at the end gives it more salience within the slogan. The positive evaluation associated with that language – and elicited through its final position in the sentence – is transferred into the evaluation of the slogan as a whole. Interestingly, these results occur irrespectively of the number of words written in the two languages and seem to be affected only by the codeswitching direction, which the authors named the *codeswitching direction effect*. As to the possible generalisation of this effect to other linguistic minorities, scholars will have to take into consideration how broadly language attitudes can vary across different communities within a country as well as in other countries. That is, negative attitudes toward Spanish within the Hispanic community might be true at this specific historical juncture in the US (Grin 1994; Koslow, Shamdasani and Touchstone 1994), but they are liable to change over time and might already be different in dissimilar contexts.

The same study points out that when attitudes toward the minority language are positive, the codeswitching direction effect no longer occurs. In fact, when respondents were induced to focus on the importance of minority languages through a stimulus devised for the purpose – thereby temporarily enhancing their attitude toward the minority language – codeswitching was perceived positively with no regard to which language came first. Therefore, arguably "the impact of codeswitching seems to depend on the direction of the code switch" (Luna and Peracchio 2005b: 53), but the real orienting factors are language attitudes.

Moreover, when assessing language attitudes in codeswitching it seems that we should analyse not only attitudes toward languages but also attitudes toward codeswitching. Research has amply proven that, generally speaking, language mixing is strongly censored both by monolinguals and multilinguals. As highlighted also by studies based on the analysis of advertisements (e.g. Bhatia 2001), if the audience holds negative attitudes toward codeswitching, then its use in advertising is not advisable since that would lead to negative outcomes. There are multilinguals, however, who have a positive or at least neutral attitude toward codeswitching, which they see as a normal practice in many circumstances (cf. Kulick and Stroud 2010: 205). In such cases, codeswitching may be helpful to advertisers who understand the potential of multilingualism and want to reach that "linguistic accommodation, which is a key ingredient for gaining maximum appeal for the product in terms of creating favourable affective consequences" (Bhatia and Ritchie 2006: 515). Still, they will have to be careful about the direction of codeswitching, as not even positive attitudes toward it seem to offset the negative impact of majority-to-minority direction (Luna and Peracchio 2005b: 47).

What can really reverse the codeswitching direction effect are positive attitudes toward both languages employed. According to the study by Luna and Peracchio, this can be partially predicted if three variables are known: strength of ethnic identification, use of codeswitching in everyday life and presence of multilingualism in the media in which the advertising is embedded. More specifically, the prevalence of one language over another in particular media is crucial when choosing the type of codeswitching. For instance, if a code-switched ad is inserted in a magazine that is mostly in English but occasionally code switches to Spanish, the ad should echo that pattern of language use. On the other hand, if the magazine is written mostly in Spanish and occasionally switches to English, the ad should switch from Spanish to English (Luna and Peracchio 2005b: 54).

In essence, multilinguals react favourably to a specific codeswitching direction if that direction is perceived as not deviating from the norm.[4]

The doctoral dissertation by Melissa Bishop (2006) provides an example of a comprehensive study on how codeswitching works in a discrete segment of the US market, the Mexican-American youth. The author further explores the importance of language salience in codeswitching, proposing that a language can become more salient in two ways: by being put at the end of a codeswitched sentence, or by being the 'other' language in a monolingual medium. Either way, the language that stands out is recalled better. Interestingly, this study, differently from studies previously published (e.g. Luna and Peracchio 2005a), does not explore language attitudes and their potential transference of positive associations to the perception of the entire advertisement, but instead focuses mainly on message recall. Results show not only that salience improves recall but also that in certain conditions codeswitching can be a "double-edged sword [. . .]. In particular, if the advertiser uses Spanish-to-English codeswitching in an all-Spanish medium context, the codeswitched text evidences better recall but the remainder of the ad message has lower recall" (Bishop 2006: 98). After analysing the various possible combinations of codeswitching directions and media language, Bishop argues that the best way to address this segment is to codeswitch from English to Spanish in an all-English medium. The study also confirms that attitudes toward codeswitching play a crucial role in determining message evaluations, variables that are further analysed in a subsequent work (Bishop 2010), in which attitudes toward codeswitching are found to be determined by the reciprocal influences of language of the media and codeswitching direction. According to this study, viewing a codeswitched advertisement in an all-Spanish language medium is negatively related to attitudes toward codeswitching, while a codeswitched advertisement – especially if English to Spanish – can be effective when placed in an all-English medium. In turn, these enhanced attitudes can positively contribute toward attaining some of the goals of advertising, such as cognitive involvement, service quality expectations and patronage intentions.

Another study by Bishop, with Peterson as a co-author, leads to some robust findings that confirm the major impact of the language of the media on the effect of codeswitching direction (Bishop and Peterson 2010). When targeting Mexican-Americans in the US, the direction of codeswitching should take into account the language of the medium in which print advertising is published. Specifically, if the language of the medium is English, the codeswitching direction should be from English to Spanish, whereas it should be the contrary if the language of the medium is Spanish. Through path analysis, Bishop and Peterson were able to demonstrate that devising advertisements that follow the codeswitching direction mentioned above leads not only to improved recall of codeswitched elements but also to perceiving the advertiser as more culturally sensitive toward the ethnic community. Such perception will, in turn, result in higher cognitive involvement in the advertisement and ultimately in more effective persuasion. The insights offered here are extremely important both in experimental and theoretical terms, as they remark how some codeswitching models, such as the Matrix Language Frame Model by Myers-Scotton and the accommodation theory, also operate in codeswitched advertising. Nevertheless, it is sensible that these results "should not be extrapolated to all bilingual Hispanics, as only Mexican-Americans within a defined age group were recruited for the study" (*ibid*: 64).

Some of these points are relevant to advertising and multilingual repertoires as explored in this volume. In particular, as it will be explained, also in my data both language attitudes and deviation or non-deviation from the linguistic norm of the media in which advertising is placed are found to be at play.

2.4 Toward an understanding of effective linguistic strategies in advertising targeting multilinguals

Studying advertising and multilingual repertoires means to explore not only the tactics employed to target multilingual audiences and the structural forces that govern multilingualism in society but also how multilinguals respond to linguistic choices that serve marketing goals.

Experimental setups have in many ways helped to understand what happens beyond the level of single advertisements or a homogenous campaign and have illuminated on key paths used by multilinguals to decode messages that use their languages. We have come to know that mental associations, emotions and schemata associated with different languages have an impact on response to advertising. In other words, in a multilingual mind, different languages carry with them a series of attributes that make a difference as far as evaluation of messages is concerned. We have also appreciated that the ease of processing of L1 versus L2 advertisements, i.e. the language effect, is a pivotal mechanism shaping patterns of response, although variables such as proficiency, dominance and fluency have been measured in different ways across studies. It has also been ascertained that the ease of processing of a dominant language is even more evident when this dominance is linked to language domains.

Moreover, as will be further discussed also in the following chapters, it is becoming increasingly clear that codeswitched advertising can be a useful tool for advertisers trying to reach multilinguals. Since codeswitching is a common practice among people who live with more than one language, using it in advertising can be perceived as an accommodation effort and thus result in positive evaluations. However, important moderators of these patterns of response are to be taken into account: the direction of codeswitching and its adherence norms, attitudes toward codeswitching and, more generally, language attitudes.

The picture, however, is still blurred. Scholars have not concentrated enough on the complexity of the multilingualism of the samples involved in their studies. In general, the accounts and subsequent classification of multilingual participants in many studies have focused on few variables, variously combined in order to obtain a general measurement of multilingualism. More broadly, as I have argued elsewhere (Santello 2015), the societal features of multilingualism have been underestimated, in favour of individual descriptors only partly in line with the holistic approach to multilingualism strongly advocated by linguists (Cenoz 2013: 10–14).

Altogether the studies in this subfield find their strength in being empirically grounded. In spite of the heterogeneity of their approaches, researchers have striven to identify a set of instruments capable of accounting for the effectiveness of language use in advertising. In particular, they have acknowledged that response to advertising is a complex phenomenon (cf. also Bhatia 2000: 117–19) that can be efficaciously gauged through a combination of tools. One of these tools is advertising evaluation, a multi-item scale that has been repeatedly used by researchers and demonstrated strong reliability (Luna and Peracchio 2005b; Bishop 2006; Carroll 2008; Carroll and Luna 2011). The scale, which encompasses questions related to liking, pleasantness, satisfaction and favourability, has often been combined with another identical scale that tests the evaluation of the product/service advertised. Such a combination of the two scales is rather significant, for research has shown that attitudes toward advertisements are conceptually different from attitudes toward products (see Klein, Ettenson and Morris 1998 for an example of the usage of attitudes toward products). However, measures of attitudes toward advertisement have been found to impact on preference and loyalty to brands (Russell and Lane 1996), and thus these measures still hold currency in the field. Moreover, measures of perceived effectiveness of communication associated with advertising messages have been utilised to obtain a more comprehensive understanding of audience response (Leclerc, Schmitt and Dubé 1994). Similarly, operationalisations of clarity of advertisements (Puntoni, De Langhe and Van Osselaer 2009; Planken, Meurs and Radlinska 2010) have been shown to function as a complement to the measurement of advertising evaluation in order to better gauge response. Most interestingly, behavioural measurements of response such as referral intention, which are more directly in line with marketing goals, have yielded rich results (Bishop and Peterson 2011). In this book I combine these instruments in order to obtain a clearer picture of patterns of response.

Notes

1 It seems that by language ability the study refers to what elsewhere is defined as self-reported language proficiency.
2 It is important to say that some results emerging from these studies – such as highly motivated participants recording lower scores of recognition of L1 advertisements compared to moderately motivated participants in the same condition – have yet to be explained.
3 In this field a major variable that seems not homogeneous throughout the studies is what constitutes codeswitching: one-word or more-than-one-word codeswitching.
4 This conclusion seems consistent with both Myers-Scotton's markedness model and Giles's accommodation theory.

References

Auer, Peter. 2002. *Code-Switching in Conversation: Language, Interaction and Identity*. New York: Routledge.
Bhatia, Tej K. 2000. *Advertising in Rural India: Language, Marketing Communication, and Consumerism*. Tokyo: Tokyo Univeristy of Foreign Studies.
Bhatia, Tej K. 2001. Language Mixing in Global Advertising. In Edwin Thumboo (ed.) *The Three Circles of English*. Singapore: Singapore University Press. 195–215.
Bhatia, Tej K., and William C. Ritchie. 2006. Bilingualism in the Global Media and Advertising. In Tej K. Bhatia and William C. Ritchie (eds.) *The Handbook of Bilingualism*. Malden, MA: Blackwell Publishing. 513–16.
Bishop, Melissa. 2006. The Role of Language Codeswitching in Increasing Advertising Effectiveness among Mexican-American Youth. PhD Thesis. Arlington: The University of Texas at Arlington.
Bishop, Melissa. 2010. The Placement of Code-Switched Ads within a Medium: Investigating Reciprocal Effects of Ad and Media Involvement. *Advances in Consumer Research* 37: 759–61.
Bishop, Melissa, and Mark Peterson. 2010. The Impact of Medium Context on Bilingual Consumers' Responses to Code-Switched Advertising. *Journal of Advertising* 39: 55–67.
Bishop, Melissa, and Mark Peterson. 2011. Comprende Code Switching? Young Mexican-Americans' Responses to Language Alternation in Print Advertising. *Journal of Advertising Research* 51: 648–59.
Blom, Jan-Petter, and John J. Gumperz. 2000. Social Meaning in Linguistic Structure: Code-Switching in Norway. In Li Wei (ed.) *The Bilingualism Reader*. London: Routledge. 102–26.

Bullo, Stella. 2014. *Evaluation in Advertising Reception: A Socio-Cognitive and Linguistic Perspective*. Houndsmill: Palgrave Macmillan.

Carroll, Ryall. 2008. The Influence of Language on Communication and Persuasion in Advertising. PhD Thesis. New York: City University of New York.

Carroll, Ryall, and David Luna. 2011. The Other Meaning of Fluency: Content Accessibility and Language in Advertising to Bilinguals. *Journal of Advertising* 40: 73–84.

Caruana, Albert, and Monica Abdilla. 2005. To Dub or Not to Dub: Language Adaptation of Global Television Advertisements for a Bilingual Community. *Journal of Brand Management* 12: 236–49.

Cenoz, Jasone. 2013. Defining Multilingualism. *Annual Review of Applied Linguistics* 33: 3–18.

de Bres, Julia. 2010. Promoting a Minority Language to Majority Language Speakers: Television Advertising about the Māori Language Targeting Non-Māori New Zealanders. *Journal of Multilingual and Multicultural Development* 31: 515–29.

Fishman, Joshua A. 1964. Language Maintenance and Language Shift as a Field of Inquiry: A Definition of the Field and Suggestions for Its Further Development. *Linguistics* 9: 32–70.

Gardner-Chloros, Penelope. 2009. *Code-Switching*. Cambridge: Cambridge University Press.

Giles, Howard, Nicholas Coupland, and Justine Coupland. 1991. Accommodation Theory: Communication, Context, and Consequences. In Howard Giles, Nicholas Coupland and Justine Coupland (eds.) *Contexts of Accommodation: Developments in Applied Sociolinguistics*. Cambridge: Cambridge University Press. 1–68.

Giles, Howard, et al. 1979. *Language and Social Psychology*. Baltimore, MD: University Park Press.

Green, Corliss L. 1999. Ethnic Evaluations of Advertising: Interaction Effects of Strength of Ethnic Identification, Media Placement, and Degree of Racial Composition. *Journal of Advertising* 28: 49–64.

Grin, François. 1994. The Bilingual Advertising Decision. *Journal of Multilingual and Multicultural Development* 15: 269–92.

Grosjean, François. 2010. *Bilingual: Life and Reality*. Cambridge: Harvard University Press.

Hmensa, Patience Afrakoma. 2010. Radio Advertising Research: A Triangular Design Perspective from an African Context. *Communication Journal of New Zealand* 11: 54–70.

Hooft, Andreu van, and Tuiet P. Truong. 2012. Language Choice and Persuasiveness. The Effects of the Use of English in Product Advertisements in Hong Kong. In Priscilla Heynderickx, et al. (eds.) *The Language Factor in International Business: New Perspectives on Research, Teaching and Practice*. Bern: Peter Lang. 175–97.

Klein, Jill G., Richard Ettenson, and Marlene D. Morris. 1998. The Animosity Model of Foreign Product Purchase: An Empirical Test in the People's Republic of China. *The Journal of Marketing* 62: 89–100.

Koslow, Scott, Prem N. Shamdasani, and Ellen E. Touchstone. 1994. Exploring Language Effects in Ethnic Advertising: A Sociolinguistic Perspective. *Journal of Consumer Research* 20: 575–85.

Kroll, Judith F., and Erika Stewart. 1994. Category Interference in Translation and Picture Naming: Evidence for Asymmetric Connections between Bilingual Memory Representations. *Journal of Memory and Language* 33: 149–74.

Kulick, Don, and Christopher Stroud. 2010. Code-Switching in Gapun: Social and Linguistic Aspects of Language Use in a Language Shifting Community. In Erik Schleef and Miriam Meyerhoff (eds.) *The Routledge Sociolinguistics Reader*. London: Routledge. 188–200.

Leclerc, France, Bernd H. Schmitt, and Laurette Dubé. 1994. Foreign Branding and Its Effects on Product Perceptions and Attitudes. *Journal of Marketing Research* 31: 263–70.

Li Wei. 2000. *The Bilingualism Reader*. London: Routledge.

Li Wei. 2005. "How Can You Tell?": Towards a Common Sense Explanation of Conversational Code-Switching. *Journal of Pragmatics* 37: 375–89.

Li Wei. 2011. Multilinguality, Multimodality, and Multicompetence: Code- and Modeswitching by Minority Ethnic Children in Complementary Schools. *The Modern Language Journal* 95: 370–84.

Luna, David. 2004. Language Processing, Affect, and Cognition: Word and Sentence Structure Effects across Languages. *Advances in Consumer Research* 31: 148–51.

Luna, David. 2011. Advertising to the Buy-Lingual Consumer. In Vivian Cook and Benedetta Bassetti (eds.) *Language and Bilingual Cognition*. Hove: Psychology. 543–58.

Luna, David, Dawn Lerman, and Laura Peracchio. 2005a. Structural Constraints in Code-Switched Advertising. *Journal of Consumer Research* 32: 416–23.

Luna, David, Dawn Lerman, and Laura Peracchio. 2005b. Structural Constraints in Mixed Language Ads: A Psycholinguistic Analysis of the Persuasiveness of Codeswitching. *Advances in Consumer Research* 32: 647–48.

Luna, David, and Laura Peracchio. 2001. Moderators of Language Effects in Advertising to Bilinguals: A Psycholinguistic Approach. *Journal of Consumer Research* 28: 284–95.

Luna, David, and Laura Peracchio. 2002. "Where There Is a Will . . .": Motivation as a Moderator of Language Processing by Bilingual Consumers. *Psychology & Marketing* 19: 573–93.

Luna, David, and Laura Peracchio. 2003. Motivation and Language Processing in Advertising to Bilingual Consumers. *Advances in Consumer Research* 30: 352–53.

Luna, David, and Laura Peracchio. 2004. Language in Multicultural Advertising: Words and Cognitive Structure. In Jerom D. Williams, Wei-Na Lee and Curtis P. Haugtvedt (eds.) *Diversity in Advertising: Broadening the Scope of Research Directions*. Mahwah, NJ: Erlbaum. 153–76.

Luna, David, and Laura Peracchio. 2005a. Advertising to Bilingual Consumers: The Impact of Code-Switching on Persuasion. *Journal of Consumer Research* 31: 760–65.

Luna, David, and Laura Peracchio. 2005b. Sociolinguistic Effects on Code-Switched Ads Targeting Bilingual Consumers. *Journal of Advertising* 34: 43–56.

Luna, David, Laura Peracchio, and Maria Dolores de Juan. 2003. The Impact of Language and Congruity on Persuasion in Multicultural E-Marketing. *Journal of Consumer Psychology* 13: 41–50.

Noriega, Jaime. 2006. Advertising to Bilinguals: Does the Language of Advertising Influence the Nature of Thoughts? PhD Thesis. Houston, TX: University of Houston.

Noriega, Jaime, and Edward Blair. 2008. Advertising to Bilinguals: Does the Language of Advertising Influence the Nature of Thoughts? *Journal of Marketing* 72: 69–83.

Planken, Brigitte, Frank van Meurs, and Ania Radlinska. 2010. The Effects of the Use of English in Polish Product Advertisements: Implications for English for Business Purposes. *English for Specific Purposes* 29: 225–42.

Poplack, Shana. 1988. Contrasting Patterns of Code-Switching in Two Communities. In Monica Heller (ed.) *Codeswitching: Anthropological and Sociolinguistic Perspectives*. New York: Mouton de Gruyter. 215–44.

Poplack, Shana. 2000. Sometimes I'll Start a Sentence in Spanish Y Termino En Español: Toward a Typology of Code-Switching. In Li Wei (ed.) *The Bilingualism Reader*. London: Routledge. 205–42.

Puntoni, Stefano, Bart De Langhe, and Stijn M. J. Van Osselaer. 2009. Bilingualism and the Emotional Intensity of Advertising Language. *Journal of Consumer Research* 35: 1012–25.

Rosignoli, Alberto. 2011. Flagging in English-Italian Code-Switching. PhD Thesis. Bangor: Bangor University.

Russell, J. Thomas, and W. Ronald Lane. 1996. *Kleppner's Advertising Procedure*. Englewood Cliffs, NJ: Prentice Hall.

Santello, Marco. 2015. Advertising to Italian English Bilinguals in Australia: Attitudes and Response to Language Selection. *Applied Linguistics* 36: 95–120.

Tavassoli, Nader T., and Yih Hwai Lee. 2003. The Differential Interaction of Auditory and Visual Advertising Elements with Chinese and English. *Journal of Marketing Research (JMR)* 40: 468–80.

Wyer, Robert S. Jr. 2002. Language and Advertising Effectiveness: Mediating Influences of Comprehension and Cognitive Elaboration. *Psychology & Marketing* 19: 693–712.

3 Studying multilingualism in advertising
Starting from lived experiences and linguistic repertoires

3.1 Toward a theoretical framework

In light of the discussion presented in the previous chapters, there seems to be a high degree of imbalance in terms of focus between studies on response and studies on texts. This is due to many factors, but conceivably the little contact between a tradition broadly aligned with marketing studies (the former) and one aligned with sociolinguistic studies (the latter) has been particularly detrimental.

In recent times attempts have been made to connect these different research traditions, as demonstrated by the insertion of a chapter written by David Luna in Cook and Bassetti's cutting-edge volume on bilingual language and cognition (Luna 2011). Likewise, on the marketing side, the growing attention to multilingual language practices demonstrates open acknowledgement of the fruitfulness of interdisciplinarity (Carroll and Luna 2011). Nevertheless, in spite of the emergence of some scattered studies that have explored the different elements that come into play in this area (Luna and Gupta 2001; Munday 2004), no harmonised theoretical framework has been established.

On the theoretical level, in this volume a first attempt is made to bridge different areas. Within this framework I study advertising by drawing upon notions based on research on multilingual campaigns (Haarmann 1989; Kelly-Holmes 2005) in a bid to find attitudinal and response correlates to what they have identified in the textual construction of advertisements. I take into consideration how symbolic and socio-psychological attributes of languages (e.g. Martin 2005; Bhatia and Ritchie 2006) could relate to the way a specific group of Italian English bilinguals in Australia react to the use of 'their' linguistic resources in advertising. Furthermore, I investigate response acknowledging 1) the complexity of response and the goals of advertising, 2) the make-up of the multilingualism of the audience, and 3) language attitudes as socio-psychological variables that are both multidimensional and localised.

With regard to response, I build upon Luna and Peracchio (2005), Bishop (2006), Luna, Ringberg and Peracchio (2008), and Carroll and Luna (2011), following a mixed method that also helps to isolate key variables that impinge on response to messages as related to linguistic strategies. I follow the seminal work of Koslow, Shamdasani and Touchstone (1994) in combining the analysis of both the characteristics of the multilingualism of the messages' recipients and their evaluation of the languages employed. Moreover, I further develop the assumptions that are centred on the relevance of symbolic values, ethnocultural stereotypes, mental associations and schemata connected to each language (e.g. Luna, Ringberg and Peracchio 2008; Puntoni, De Langhe and Van Osselaer 2009; Carroll and Luna 2011) by also exploring language attitudes.

In studying multilingualism I adopt a notion that relates to lived experience, aligned with the one proposed by Grosjean (1982; 2010), bridging a societal and an individual approach. Under this perspective, linguistic repertoires are analysed as a set of resources within a sociolinguistic context that are both individually relevant and shared with groups of speakers. Moreover, drawing upon Marian, Blumenfeld and Kaushanskaya (2007) and Baker (2006), I take up an approach to the measurement of multilingualism that considers competence measures, language use scales and language background/history questions. I focus specifically on language dominance, one of the measurement criteria that is able to account for the complexity of a multilingual life.

Language attitudes are seen as socio-psychological variables that are intrinsically multidimensional. In particular, language attitudes are defined as the range of associations in terms of language-specific dimensions people have with a language in its entirety and considering its coexistence with other languages (Santello 2015b). In other words, I consider 1) language attitudes as conceptual constructs (Coupland and Bishop 2007); 2) their multidimensionality that is consistent with but goes beyond the dimensions found in previous research (Zahn and Hopper 1985; Baker 1992); 3) their 'locality' (Edwards 1999; Buchstaller 2010); and 4) their ties with multilingualism (Myers-Scotton 2006).

Overall, in terms of methodology, the consideration of the complexity of repertoires is combined with the detailed elicitation of advertising effects.

In particular, multilingualism is studied through a range of self-reported measures that enrich and add detail to the understanding of the linguistic side of the investigation. Similarly, the identification of advertising effects benefits from two components: a qualitative context-focused investigation eliciting explicit attitudes toward language use in advertising (this chapter), a multivariate and multidimensional method that can account for advertising goals and outcomes as well as permitting greater generalisability of results (next two chapters).

My approach connects several fields of research by investigating advertising and multilingual repertoires under a linguistic perspective, allowing for the combination of multilingualism, language attitude and advertising research that could potentially provide further insights into the complex relationship between multilingualism and persuasion.

3.2 Languages in advertising as direct experiences

Following the approach described above, I organised a focus group in Sydney in order to identify the attitudes of Italian English bilinguals toward the use of Italian and English in advertising. I described the rationale behind this choice and the procedure I followed in a previous work (Santello 2015a), but here I wish to report briefly the composition of the focus group in a way that is conducive to an understanding of the new data I present herein.

I intended to create a group of informants that could generate a discussion able to bring to the surface the meaning that the use of linguistic resources creates in advertising communication when these linguistic resources are familiar to the recipients. In order to achieve this I included among the participants only individuals who considered themselves highly competent in both Italian and English and who were either born in Australia or lived in the country permanently with their families. In addition, participants would all self-identify as Italian. This element was crucial for this study because I wanted the participants to be a homogenous group of people that shared, at least to a certain degree, linguistic repertoires and cultural background. In fact numerous studies have shown that for a focus group to work, it is imperative that it be made up of individuals who share a number of traits and thus feel at ease voicing their positions in front of other members (Green and Hart 1998: 29–35; Stewart and Shamdasani 2014: 17–29). These participants were all highly educated, although only one had a PhD, and they were involved in extensive social networks within the Italian community.

In addition to putting together a homogenous group of people, it was also important to attain a degree of diversification in terms of language competence and life experiences (Kitzinger and Barbour 1998: 7–15), so I recruited both multilinguals who self-reported being English dominants and Italian dominants and decided to exclude students. I wanted individuals who were part of the actual community (Berg, Lune and Lune 2004: 158–62), who were not necessarily accustomed to reflecting on social or linguistic issues. In other words, I wanted them to be hypothetical addressees of advertising in Italian and in English.

To recruit the participants I advertised the focus group in a local Italian newspaper and on the Italian radio in Sydney. Initially I had little interest from potential participants, so I decided to add a 10AU$ gift voucher to partially cover transportation costs (Barbour 2008: 54–55). The voucher worked well, and I could quickly gather the informants I needed according to the linguistic and background criteria I had set. I gathered the eight multilingual women who agreed to participate in a room located in an Italian suburb and started the discussion offering a light refreshment. We first talked about our languages and our background and subsequently we started discussing languages in advertising. We touched upon the use of Italian in advertising in Australia, languages in mainstream advertising, language use in advertising targeting migrant communities, language choice in advertising to Italian English bilinguals, and appropriateness of language choice in addressing multilinguals according to a set of variables such as target audience, product/service advertised and language of the medium in which advertising is embedded. The participants were invited to reflect on all forms of advertising, such as TV commercials, print advertising, radio advertising and billboards.

3.3 Attitudes toward languages in advertising: Insights from Italian English speakers

Attitudes that emerge from focus group discussions can be very revealing of the functioning of languages in advertising. In my research (Santello 2015a) I have shown that languages are evaluated by these multilinguals both for their socio-psychological work and their functional one. In regard to the latter, the audience's language competence appears to be one important element for language choice to be considered appropriate. Regarding the former, the connotations of the languages seem to complement and intersect the appraisal of the audience's repertoire, thus playing a role in this multilingual group.

The data presented here further report on the articulation of attitudes toward languages in advertising, with a specific focus on the localised nature of these attitudes as they emerge in interaction. The excerpts are presented as talk (Myers and Macnaghten 1998) and interpreted in light of the conversational context in which they are generated (Burningham 1995; Waterton and Wynne 1998). I take care to identify not only the topics around which each excerpt revolves and how the co-construction of arguments is carried out (Bloor et al. 2001: 59–72; Puchta and Potter 2004: 142–61) but also the participants' positioning vis-à-vis the moderator and other group members. In the first extract I report a short exchange among group members around the choice of English versus Italian in advertising to multilinguals.

Extract 1

Participant 1:	Sulla *Fiamma* many ads are in English.
Participant 2:	Because they are probably trying to get the collaterals . . .
Participant 3:	Quelli sulle tombe sono in inglese.
Participant 4:	That's because they are the children that have to organise everything.
Participant 2:	That's right, exactly.

English Translation

Participant 1:	*In* La Fiamma *many ads are in English.*
Participant 2:	*Because they are probably trying to get the collaterals . . .*
Participant 3:	*Funeral homes ads are in English.*
Participant 4:	*That's because they are the children that have to organise everything.*
Participant 2:	*That's right, exactly.*

In this extract four different multilinguals are discussing their direct experiences with language use in advertising. Participant 1 introduces the local newspaper where advertisements are published, making salient her own recollection of language use. Although *La Fiamma* regularly hosts entire pages written in English, it is predominantly in Italian and generally perceived as an Italian-language medium. The participant implies that the language of advertising does not match the language of the medium, which is explained by participant 2 as a strategy to target a specific audience. In these statements we can already trace some correlates to what researchers have argued based on textual analysis: language choice is here an instrument to target specific audiences, serving as a target segmentation tool (Kelly-Holmes 2005: 108–16). The expectation would be that advertisements in Italian should be there if the medium is in Italian, but the participants' direct experiences with language use are misaligned with this broad assumption: in the newspaper readers can also find advertisements in English. The collaterals of older Italians are addressed in English and, as the discussion goes on, examples are made as to when the language is chosen and what lies behind the choice. Funeral homes design their advertisements in English because the target is made up of the kids of those who died, that is, younger family members who are competent in English. The direct experiences with the languages inform the attitudes voiced by the multilinguals. What we notice here is the creation of a discourse dynamic that both reflects and enacts a number of contradictions and tensions, in this case manifested as interplay between an understanding of the goals of advertising, particularly that of targeting different segments of the audience, and an understanding of the multilingualism of the community. The multilingualism of Italians in Australia is seen as a key element in the way advertising works and positioned alongside marketing aims. In other words, to use Bhatia's (2000) terms, the coding and decoding of messages appear to be explicitly bound together by these multilinguals. This thought is further elaborated in the following longer extract:

Extract 2

Moderator:	And let's say there's a company that on purpose chooses Italian instead of English to address an Italian in Australia, would your opinion about the company change?
Participant 7:	I have to comment on Brand3. They advertise once a week in Italian for their bridal industry. I think it's fantastic. They must have someone really good in their marketing department. That's in *La Fiamma*, it's down the bottom in black.
Moderator:	So you are thinking: "This company is actually good"?
Participant 7:	Yeah, they are doing something to go and grab that side of the market.
Participant 3:	I also think it's a good thing. I guess they would do it not only for Italian, but for the other languages too. And I think I would agree. It's a good point.

Moderator: E tu participant 5 cosa pensi?

Participant 5: I don't see any media, nessun mezzo di comunicazione
                che io usufruisco quindi non lo so cosa mi fa una
                pubblicità. Non vedo come una pubblicità italiana mi
                possa raggiungere a meno che non venga fatta da un
                grosso mezzo di comunicazione.

English translation

Moderator: *And let's say there's a company that on purpose chooses
                Italian instead of English to address an Italian in
                Australia, would your opinion about the company
                change?*

Participant 7: *I have to comment on Brand3. They advertise once
                a week in Italian for their bridal industry. I think it's
                fantastic. They must have someone really good in their
                marketing department. That's in* La Fiamma, *it's down
                the bottom in black.*

Moderator: *So you are thinking: "This company is actually good"?*

Participant 7: *Yeah, they are doing something to go and grab that side
                of the market.*

Participant 3: *I also think it's a good thing. I guess they would do it
                not only for Italian, but for the other languages too.
                And I think I would agree. It's a good point.*

Moderator: *And you, participant 5, what do you reckon?*

Participant 5: *I don't see any media, no media that I use so I wouldn't
                know what impact an ad would be on me. I don't see
                how an Italian ad could possibly reach me unless it's in
                a big medium.*

After being asked about their attitude change depending on language selection, participants resort to their recollections of campaigns. Participant 7 mentions a large Australian retail company, here anonymised, and comments on its advertisements in *La Fiamma*. She remembers exactly where the advertisements are usually placed within the layout of the newspaper and wishes to share it with the rest of the group. She is pleased that the company chooses to advertise in Italian in *La Fiamma*; in her view it is smart that Italians are targeted in their language in a newspaper aimed at them. Interestingly, instead of arguing that English should be the language chosen for the advertisement in that younger members of the community are the intended target of these bridal campaigns, she is commenting on the strategy itself without making remarks on appropriateness of language choice. She is again mentioning her experiences with advertising strategies related to one company and one advertising initiative. She does not generalise her emic view to all campaigns and all products, but cares to highlight that she is pleased with seeing a large company advertising in a community newspaper to an Italian-speaking audience. In actual fact, the observation is inchoately relaunched with an attempt to extend this assumption to other languages, but is then silenced by the statement of participant 5. She claims not to be reached by advertisements of any sort and thus cannot reflect upon languages in advertising. By refusing to comment on these issues and actively deflecting the moderator's request (Medved and Brockmeier 2015: 92–94), she is making salient something shared with other participants, i.e. the need to formulate statements based on lived experiences (cf. Busch 2013). It is their being touched by languages in advertising that allows these multilinguals to shape their accounts whereby their 'personal attitudes toward language can be framed' (Busch 2015: 9).

In the following passage I try to induce them to make more general conclusions and to look at the bigger picture:

Extract 3

Moderator:	Okay, very well. Now, how would you feel if someone is addressing you in Italian as an Italian in Australia? Let's say you are walking around Five Dock and there is a billboard in Italian. How would you feel? That the billboard is in Italian instead of English?
Participant 8:	Fantastico.
Participant 1:	Yeah, special.
Participant 7:	You can even practice if you are not Italian, because it's going to be there for a few days.
Participant 4:	No, sono contenta. Poi forse mi sbaglio e dico: "Ma è scritto sale [Italian] o sale [English]?" [Laughter]
Participant 7:	When I see Italy in the backdrop of magazines, I think it's fantastic. I am proud that my parents were Italian.
Participant 5:	Stavo pensando alla prima volta che sono andata a Haberfield e ho visto il cartello di Piazza della Federazione in italiano e in inglese. Era come un modo di marcare Haberfield come italiana.

English translation

Moderator:	Okay, very well. Now, how would you feel if someone is addressing you in Italian as an Italian in Australia? Let's say you are walking around Five Dock and there is a billboard in Italian. How would you feel? That the billboard is in Italian instead of English?
Participant 8:	Fantastic.
Participant 1:	Yeah, special.
Participant 7:	You can even practice if you are not Italian, because it's going to be there for a few days.
Participant 4:	Yeah, I'd be happy. Though maybe I get it wrong and think: "Does it say sale [Italian] or sale [English]?" [Laughter]
Participant 7:	When I see Italy in the backdrop of magazines, I think it's fantastic. I am proud that my parents were Italian.
Participant 5:	I was thinking about one time I went to Haberfield and saw a sign in Federation Square in Italian and English. It was like a way to mark Haberfield as Italian.

With my question I try to shift their attention from *La Fiamma* to other forms of advertising. I intend to see whether the participants are willing to make their attitudes more generalised instead of referring exclusively to their recollections. My attempt is initially well received when several participants agree to consider the hypothetical situation of walking around Little Italy and seeing a billboard in Italian. Participant 4 jokes about her multilingualism and potential misunderstandings with Italian homographs of English nouns, and participant 7 refers to passersby unintentionally reached by messages in Italian. However, it seems that here some members of the group are also fairly disoriented, as is the case of participant 7, who mentions the use of Italy in advertising instead of focusing on languages. While reinforcing the strict association between a country of origin and the use of a language (Martin 2005), the statement deviates from the central topic. The exchange then ends once again with a reference to a familiar place and something seen in real life, the multilingual sign of a square in a suburb of the city. The discussion points toward symbolic values of languages and builds upon the participants' knowledge of the community, its spaces and its linguascape (Giampapa 2004: 197–200).

In spite of my attempts to open a discussion on hypothetical situations, links to lived experiences of language are still central for the construction of attitudes in this group discussion. Putative scenarios avulsed from contextualised occurrences of language seem to lead to digressions and disoriented behaviour or, at least, render the discussion less cohesive. Off-topic remarks are still useful for the understating of the socio-psychological factors at work in the process of attitude formation (Bullo 2014: 120–29) and can hardly be avoided in any case. Most interestingly, though, they signal some form of uneasiness with abstract conjectures and corroborate a contextualised development of attitudes toward languages in advertising. Extract 4 exemplifies the experiential foundation of these 'attitudes in interaction' (Liebscher and Dailey-O'Cain 2009) and expands on the symbolic work of languages.

Extract 4

Participant 7:   Brand1 used the accent only, for example. [. . .]
*Participant 6:   And Brand2's had one where they were speaking only
                  Italian and it wasn't as good as the Brand1 one. I am
                  Italian and I can understand but other people wouldn't
                  and I don't think it had that appeal.*

When asked to comment on linguistic resources in advertising, a number of times participants instinctively referred also to the use of Italian in mainstream advertising targeting both Italians and non-Italians. In particular, they referred to the use of Italian as a second language, i.e. together with English, in general advertising, and assessed its use according to different levels of appropriateness. As evident in extract 4, participants are aware that there are differences in how communication is established when advertisers make a choice about language. Commenting on two different campaigns of pasta sauce, they propose a distinction between using an Italian accent or the language itself. Moreover, participants establish a direct link between language choice and linguistic competence of the audience, further connecting it to effectiveness. What is noticeable here is also a discourse that embodies a separation between the general audience and Italian speakers in Australia, whereby non-speakers are othered on linguistic grounds (Riggins 1997). Audiences are here imagined as non-speakers of Italian, and their being reached by different forms of language use is contingent on their ability to understand. In actual fact, comments on the choice and the use of Italian to target non-multilinguals seem informed by the recognition of its socio-psychological features, as described by Bhatia and Ritchie (2006), in the sense of characteristics of the language that can be used to generate meaning in advertising. This occurrence is to be linked also to the exploitation of ethnocultural stereotypes (Haarmann 1989) typical of ethnosymbolism.

Extract 5

Participant 1: Beh, su Rete Italia è molto in italiano, praticamente tutto in italiano.

Participant 2: I want to say that if something is in English it stands out. I'm not saying it's good, I'm not saying it's bad, but maybe because I was born here I would go like: "Oh, that's in English".

Participant 4: To me if I read *La Fiamma* and I see an English ad, it would stand out because I'm reading everything in Italian. So I'm thinking: "Wow, that's English".

Moderator: How about if you are listening to SBS?

Participant 4: Yeah. Just because obviously, if my brain is working that I'm listening to Italian, and then all of a sudden I hear English, it captures me and I go, okay, what's going on? Well, I don't know how much of attention I would pay to it, in the sense that maybe I am not interested in the ad and after two seconds I am not listening to it anymore.

English translation

Participant 1: *Well, on Rete Italia a lot is in Italian, basically everything is in Italian.*

Participant 2: *I want to say that if something is in English it stands out. I'm not saying it's good, I'm not saying it's bad, but maybe because I was born here I would go like: "Oh, that's in English".*

Participant 4: *To me if I read* La Fiamma *and I see an English ad, it would stand out because I'm reading everything in Italian. So I'm thinking: "Wow, that's English".*

Moderator: *How about if you are listening to SBS?*

Participant 4: *Yeah. Just because obviously, if my brain is working that I'm listening to Italian, and then all of a sudden I hear English, it captures me and I go, okay, what's going on? Well, I don't know how much of attention*

> *I would pay to it, in the sense that maybe I am not*
> *interested in the ad and after two seconds I am not*
> *listening to it anymore.*

What emerges from extract 5 is something akin to what Bishop and Peterson (2010; 2011) have found through experimental methods. Languages used in advertising do not stand in a vacuum, but they are in a dialectical relationship with the media in which they appear. There seem to be two key factors that these multilinguals take into consideration. On one side it is the prevalence of one language within a specific media space, which determines a set of expectations against which multilingual audiences assess language choice. On the other side, participants show awareness of the cognitive processes that are implied by moving abruptly from one language to another when reading. Participant 4 states that when her brain is working in Italian a sudden language change may attract her attention to the advertisement. She also reports that this cognitive shift does not necessarily translate into effectiveness or memorability. Remarkably, then, not only do some of these multilinguals seem to be aware that language selection can be used as a tool in advertising above and beyond its usefulness as an audience segmentation tool, they are also cognisant of the complexity of advertising goals, a very important element to be considered in research on advertising in multilingual contexts. I have already discussed how considering the plurality of goals that advertisers set in response to marketing strategies is key for a comprehensive understanding of the sense-making of advertising in multilingual settings. It seems that among these Italian English multilinguals such understanding is already 'brought in' (Andrews 2015: 45–46) when assessing language use in concrete situations. Participant 4 makes a distinction between enhanced attention toward a message and recall of the content, two important elements that I take into consideration in my study. Looking more closely at extract 4, therefore, attitudes toward language use in advertising show interconnections between the expectations in terms of language choice that the audience has built up over time and the multilingual cognitive processes of the addressee. In Chapter 4 and Chapter 5 I will make specific allowance for the possible correlation of collateral variables with response to advertising, testing whether the use of linguistic resources has the power to increase perceived effectiveness of advertising in an experimental setting.

Extract 6 provides another instance of the complexity of response in the eyes of the participants and the amount of factors that may come into play.

Extract 6

Participant 3:   An issue of La Fiamma *is in English. I think it's on
                   Wednesdays.*

Participant 2:   *I guess with ads I think they are marketing to lots
                   of different people at the same time, trying to catch
                   different people, maybe, at the same time. And
                   probably, this discussion, we are disagreeing on this
                   point is symptomatic of what they are trying to achieve,
                   which is . . . try to get that person, try to get that
                   person . . . and it would react to some it won't react to
                   others.*

Participant 6:   *And it depends on what the product is, too. If they
                   are advertising scooter things, and it's a Vespa or
                   Lambretta and it has got something Italian, like Italian
                   people or Italian messages, it lends itself to something
                   Italian, then it's appropriate. The same is for a coffee
                   percolator.*

Moderator: *Right. And would it be appropriate for something
                   technical like a washing machine? If the ad is on La
                   Fiamma?*

Participant 6:   *For me, I read La Fiamma, because I want to read
                   Italian. But I take the point that other people want to
                   see it in English. For me it's appropriate if it is the
                   Italian radio station, it's all in Italian.*

Participant 1:   *Well, if you are to buy something technical like a
                   washing machine and you are comparing different
                   products, you don't want a translation because it can be
                   ambiguous. I think you want to see it in English.*

Moderator: *For clarity, you mean?*

Participant 1:   *Yes.*

Participant 2:   *Yes.*

At the beginning of the exchange what emerges is the sense that these
participants see clearly the link between language use and marketing strategies. They have considered various aspects relating to the choice and the
use of Italian and English in a number of possible permutations and seem
to share the idea that not only advertising goals are manifold but also audiences are. Depending on the characteristics of the audiences, language use

may or may not be successfully received. Participant 6 adds to this the possibility that companies would want to advertise products that are 'marked' (Johnson 2012: 103) as Italian in the marketplace, such as Vespas or Lambrettas. Products would be branded and appropriated as Italian thanks also to the language, here clearly associated with cultural meanings. Symbolic and socio-psychological attributes of languages are once again put front and centre, this time ever more clearly in relation with an understanding of language in advertising as fetish, broadly in line with textual analysis of advertising (Kelly-Holmes 2005).

This association between specific kinds of products and language use has been found particularly important in previous studies (Haarmann 1989: 99–116; Piller 2003: 171–73), so I try to elicit more comments on this topic. Once again, instead of making general statements, participants link their attitudes to known media settings, like local newspapers and radio stations, expanding on the expectations these media have built together with the audience. Lived experiences drive them through the complexity of language choice. Participant 6, in particular, does not see the point of shifting language from Italian into English for advertising when audiences are choosing a programme expressly because it is in Italian. However, she also sees that her position is not shared by everybody in the group and accepts this diversification, similarly to what participant 2 did at the beginning of the exchange.

The final turns touch upon a rather underexplored topic in advertising to multilingual audiences, which is the type of product advertised and the influence of decision-taking routes behind their evaluation by consumers. I cannot elaborate on this point with the necessary depth here, but I still wish to include this element as an additional instantiation of the concreteness and everydayness of the evaluation of advertising within the life of individuals living in multilingual contexts. For participant 1 it is not trivial whether the product would need to be compared carefully to others and how language choice may impede or facilitate a sensible purchase. She wishes that language choice did not interfere with her making a good choice when buying a washing machine. According to the Elaboration Likelihood Model (Petty and Cacioppo 1986; Petty, Wegener and Fabrigar 1997), one of the main ways individuals process advertising centrally[1] is by comparing products or services before purchasing them. In order for the comparison to be carried out with ease, the way information on products is conveyed needs to be consistent across advertisements. Given that most advertising in Australia is in English, when a possible comparison among products is deemed important, participant 1 seems to opt for keeping English in all circumstances.

3.4 Understanding the side of the addressee

If we intend to fill the gap between studies concerned with multilingual textual construction and those interested in the response mechanisms on the side of the addressee, a possible starting point is a better understanding of the tensions between language use and the multilingualism of the audience that advertising reaches. In this chapter I have shown a first step toward this kind of understanding, adopting an approach that starts from attitudes toward language use in context and allows the plurality of interconnections between messages, repertoires and additional marketing factors to emerge. I have noted that speakers of Italian and English in Australia tap into their direct experiences with the languages to form their attitudes. These experiences span from language use in society, difference in competence between speakers, expectations connected with the media that have been built through time, characteristics of the product advertised and other references to familiar 'encounters' (Goodwin and Duranti 1992) with languages in marketing discourse. Participants do not shy away from acknowledging the conflicting trajectories of language use and of attitudes toward them, but rather demonstrate a heightened awareness of both marketing purposes and linguistic stratification in both messages and society. Their lived experiences place them in a position where they can formulate fine-grained views and bring in a number of elements that could potentially be overlooked when advertising in multilingual contexts does not account for the decoding side of communication, as Bhatia (2000: 3) would say. Moreover, it could be argued that textual analysis alone may underestimate the multifarious spectrum of marketing goals that advertising sets as its final strategic point. Nevertheless, in several instances declarative data have largely paralleled what has been found in previous research, signalling in many ways its validity and applicability.

In fact, investigating advertising in multilingual contexts through focus groups means that we can unveil the work of linguistic resources from the inside. Multilinguals, for instance, are able to enucleate some of the dialectic connections between psycholinguistic and purchase-related routes to persuasion as they perceive them against the backdrop of language use. They can also bring to the fore the connotations of linguistic strategies when these strategies transit from their source to their recipients, touching upon their perceived effectiveness according to various kinds of audiences and their linguistic as well as demographic characteristics. On condition that speakers are selected in order to generate a convivial atmosphere that is also conducive to the arousal of divergences, this form of group discussions is capable of mapping some remarkable tensions between linguistic resources in localised marketing settings and possible decoding pathways followed by speakers, in a way that both clarifies some issues and problematises others. While this investigation has explained that socio-psychological features originate from the knowledge of the sociolinguistic environment that multilinguals experience, it has also posed questions regarding the expectations on the use of linguistic resources in advertising that speakers build over time. In other words, the multilayered core of response comes to light to show its experiential base as well as its projected connotations.

These new insights into the dynamics at play at the decoding end of multilingual advertising communication are theoretically significant in that they can possibly connect the existence of discursive trends on a global and local scale to the linguistic life of audiences. In doing that, the construction of campaigns can enter into dialogue with its audience counterpart and start adding details to the social and individual factors that shape multilingualism in advertising. The next chapters will attempt to outline an approach that includes societal elements of multilingualism, their interconnectedness with language as it is used in messages and the nature of advertising as a marketing tool oriented toward commercial objectives.

Note

1 Consumers use advertising as a tool to take decisions on purchases: this decision-making process can be conscious (central route of processing) or unconscious (peripheral route of processing). Central processes occur more often with products or services that require motivation for high thought, such as expensive goods like motor vehicles, real estate or appliances. Peripheral processes tend to prevail when low motivation for thinking is involved, which is often the case of relatively unimportant and inexpensive goods like confectionary or stationary.

References

Andrews, Molly. 2015. The Nice Stasi Man Drove His Trabi to the Nudist Beach: Contesting East German Identity. In Roberta Piazza and Alessandra Fasulo (eds.) *Marked Identities: Narrating Lives between Social Labels and Individual Biographies*. Houndmills, Basingstoke, Hampshire: Palgrave Macmillan. 43–57.
Baker, Colin. 1992. *Attitudes and Language*. Clevedon: Multilingual Matters.
Baker, Colin. 2006. *Foundations of Bilingual Education and Bilingualism*. Clevedon: Multilingual Matters.
Barbour, Rosaline. 2008. *Doing Focus Groups*. London; Thousand Oaks, CA: Sage.

Berg, Bruce Lawrence, Howard Lune, and Howard Lune. 2004. *Qualitative Research Methods for the Social Sciences.* Boston.

Bhatia, Tej K. 2000. *Advertising in Rural India: Language, Marketing Communication, and Consumerism.* Tokyo: Tokyo Univeristy of Foreign Studies.

Bhatia, Tej K., and William C. Ritchie. 2006. Bilingualism in the Global Media and Advertising. In Tej K. Bhatia and William C. Ritchie (eds.) *The Handbook of Bilingualism.* Malden, MA: Blackwell Publishing. 513–16.

Bishop, Melissa. 2006. The Role of Language Codeswitching in Increasing Advertising Effectiveness among Mexican-American Youth. PhD Thesis. Arlington: The University of Texas at Arlington.

Bishop, Melissa, and Mark Peterson. 2010. The Impact of Medium Context on Bilingual Consumers' Responses to Code-Switched Advertising. *Journal of Advertising* 39: 55–67.

Bishop, Melissa, and Mark Peterson. 2011. Comprende Code Switching? Young Mexican-Americans' Responses to Language Alternation in Print Advertising. *Journal of Advertising Research* 51: 648–59.

Bloor, Michael, et al. 2001. *Focus Groups in Social Research.* London; Thousand Oaks, CA: Sage.

Buchstaller, Isabelle. 2010. Social Stereotypes, Personality Traits and Regional Perception Displaced: Attitudes Towards the 'New' Quotatives in the U.K. In Erik Schleef and Miriam Meyerhoff (eds.) *The Routledge Sociolinguistics Reader.* London: Routledge. 168–82.

Bullo, Stella. 2014. *Evaluation in Advertising Reception: A Socio-Cognitive and Linguistic Perspective.* Houndsmill: Palgrave Macmillan.

Burningham, Kate. 1995. Attitudes, Accounts and Impact Assessment. *The Sociological Review* 43: 100–22.

Busch, Brigitta. 2013. *Mehrprachigkeit.* Vienna: Facultas/UTB.

Busch, Brigitta. 2015. Linguistic Repertoire and Spracherleben, the Lived Experience of Language. *Working Papers in Urban Language & Literacies* 1: 1–16.

Carroll, Ryall, and David Luna. 2011. The Other Meaning of Fluency: Content Accessibility and Language in Advertising to Bilinguals. *Journal of Advertising* 40: 73–84.

Coupland, Nikolas, and Hywel Bishop. 2007. Ideologised Values for British Accents. *Journal of Sociolinguistics* 11: 74–93.

Edwards, John. 1999. Refining Our Understanding of Language Attitudes. *Journal of Language and Social Psychology* 15: 101–10.

Giampapa, Frances. 2004. The Politics of Identity, Representation and Discourses of Self-Identification: Negotiating the Periphery and the Center. In Aneta Pavlenko and Adrian Blackledge (eds.) *Negotiation of Identities in Multilingual Contexts.* Clevedon: Multilingual Matters. 192–218.

Goodwin, Charles, and Alessandro Duranti. 1992. *Rethinking Context: Language as an Interactive Phenomenon.* Cambridge: Cambridge University Press.

Green, Judith, and Laura Hart. 1998. The Impact of Context on Data. In Rosaline Barbour and Jenny Kitzinger (eds.) *Developing Focus Group Research: Politics, Theory and Practice.* London; Thousand Oaks, CA: Sage. 21–35.

Grosjean, François. 1982. *Life with Two Languages: An Introduction to Bilingualism*. Cambridge: Harvard University Press.

Grosjean, François. 2010. *Bilingual: Life and Reality*. Cambridge: Harvard University Press.

Haarmann, Harald. 1989. *Symbolic Values of Foreign Language Use*. Berlin: Mouton de Gruyter.

Johnson, Fern. 2012. *Imaging in Advertising: Verbal and Visual Codes of Commerce*. New York: Routledge.

Kelly-Holmes, Helen. 2005. *Advertising as Multilingual Communication*. Houndmills, Basingstoke, Hampshire: Palgrave Macmillan.

Kitzinger, Jenny, and Rosaline Barbour. 1998. The Challenge and Promise of Focus Groups. In Rosaline Barbour and Jenny Kitzinger (eds.) *Developing Focus Group Research: Politics, Theory and Practice*. London; Thousand Oaks, CA: Sage. 1–20.

Koslow, Scott, Prem N. Shamdasani, and Ellen E. Touchstone. 1994. Exploring Language Effects in Ethnic Advertising: A Sociolinguistic Perspective. *Journal of Consumer Research* 20: 575–85.

Liebscher, Grit, and Jennifer Dailey-O'Cain. 2009. Language Attitudes in Interaction. *Journal of Sociolinguistics* 13: 195–222.

Luna, David. 2011. Advertising to the Buy-Lingual Consumer. In Vivian Cook and Benedetta Bassetti (eds.) *Language and Bilingual Cognition*. Hove: Psychology. 543–58.

Luna, David, and Susan Forquer Gupta. 2001. An Integrative Framework for Cross-Cultural Consumer Behavior. *International Marketing Review* 18: 45–69.

Luna, David, and Laura Peracchio. 2005. Sociolinguistic Effects on Code-Switched Ads Targeting Bilingual Consumers. *Journal of Advertising* 34: 43–56.

Luna, David, Torsten Ringberg, and Laura Peracchio. 2008. One Individual, Two Identities: Frame Switching among Biculturals. *Journal of Consumer Research* 35: 279–93.

Marian, Viorica, Henrike K. Blumenfeld, and Margarita Kaushanskaya. 2007. The Language Experience and Proficiency Questionnaire (Leap-Q): Assessing Language Profiles in Bilinguals and Multilinguals. *Journal of Speech, Language, and Hearing Research* 50: 940–67.

Martin, Elizabeth. 2005. *Marketing Identities through Language: English and Global Imagery in French Advertising*. Basingstoke: Palgrave Macmillan.

Medved, Maria I., and Jens Brockmeier. 2015. On the Margins: Aboriginal Realities and 'White Man's Research'. In Roberta Piazza and Alessandra Fasulo (eds.) *Marked Identities: Narrating Lives between Social Labels and Individual Biographies*. Houndmills, Basingstoke, Hampshire: Palgrave Macmillan. 79–97.

Munday, Jeremy. 2004. Advertising: Some Challenges to Translation Theory. *The Translator* 10: 199–219.

Myers, Greg, and Phil Macnaghten. 1998. Can Focus Groups Be Analyzed as Talk? In Rosaline Barbour and Jenny Kitzinger (eds.) *Developing Focus Group Research: Politics, Theory and Practice*. London; Thousand Oaks, CA: Sage. 173–85.

Myers-Scotton, Carol. 2006. *Multiple Voices: An Introduction to Bilingualism*. Oxford: Blackwell Publishing.

Petty, Richard E., and John T. Cacioppo. 1986. *Communication and Persuasion: Central and Peripheral Routes to Attitude Change*. New York: Springer-Verlag.

Petty, Richard E., Duane T. Wegener, and Leandre R. Fabrigar. 1997. Attitudes and Attitude Change. *Annual Review of Psychology* 48: 609–47.

Piller, Ingrid. 2003. Advertising as a Site of Language Contact. *Annual Review of Applied Linguistics* 23: 170–83.

Puchta, Claudia, and Jonathan Potter. 2004. *Focus Group Practice*. London; Thousand Oaks, CA: Sage.

Puntoni, Stefano, Bart De Langhe, and Stijn M. J. Van Osselaer. 2009. Bilingualism and the Emotional Intensity of Advertising Language. *Journal of Consumer Research* 35: 1012–25.

Riggins, Stephen Harold Ed. 1997. *The Language and Politics of Exclusion. Others in Discourse*. Thousand Oaks, CA: Sage.

Santello, Marco. 2015a. Advertising to Italian English Bilinguals in Australia: Attitudes and Response to Language Selection. *Applied Linguistics* 36: 95–120.

Santello, Marco. 2015b. Bilingual Idiosyncratic Dimensions of Language Attitudes. *International Journal of Bilingual Education and Bilingualism* 18: 1–25.

Stewart, David W., and Prem N. Shamdasani. 2014. *Focus Groups: Theory and Practice*. Thousand Oaks, CA: Sage.

Waterton, Claire, and Brian Wynne. 1998. Can Focus Groups Access Community Views? In Rosaline Barbour and Jenny Kitzinger (eds.) *Developing Focus Group Research: Politics, Theory and Practice*. London; Thousand Oaks, CA: Sage. 127–43.

Zahn, Christopher J., and Robert Hopper. 1985. Measuring Language Attitudes: The Speech Evaluation Instrument. *Journal of Language and Social Psychology* 4: 113–23.

4 Linguistic resources in advertising and their impact on multilinguals

4.1 From advertising goals to patterns of response

In a previous work (Santello 2015) I have shown that experiments are powerful instruments to understand advertising in multilingual contexts. Controlled experimental settings make it possible to verify whether multilinguals who belong to a defined group of speakers display response to language use in advertising that differs from or complements what has been found through textual analysis. Findings could even diverge from what one could predict in light of the psycholinguistic mechanisms revealed by studying Hispanics in the US. In the case of Italian English bilinguals in Australia – here referred to also as multilinguals for the sake of consistency with the rest of the volume – when exposed to advertisements in Italian or in English, the speakers tend to respond more or less positively according to their language dominance, intended as "the degree to which a bilingual leans towards one language" (Santello 2014: 26). However, as opposed to what one could expect, Italian dominants respond more favourably to advertisements in English than in Italian, while English dominants respond more favourably to advertisements in Italian. These results were obtained using a range of print advertisements – spanning different types of product categories – that were not only understandable but also structurally varied so that they produced different levels of appreciation and response.

Previous results therefore indicate that the routes along which multilinguals react to advertisements are not solely driven by language effects linked to ease of processing but also by other language-related features. Nevertheless, response was operationalised in my previous study based on two indicators, i.e. advertising evaluation and product evaluation, both comprising seven-item scales: the first aimed at assessing the evaluation of advertising in terms of liking, pleasantness, satisfaction, and favourability;

the second was identical to the first one, but aimed to elicit the evaluation of the products advertised instead of the advertisements themselves. Although the scales were drawn from previous studies, in which they proved highly reliable (Luna and Peracchio 2005a; Carroll and Luna 2011), I pointed out in Chapter 2 that advertising strategies envisage a host of goals that are variously associated with evaluation but are not equal to it. Therefore, while advertising and product evaluation are central elements in determining response, language effects on multilingual speakers can be more comprehensively gauged by also employing other measures. As discussed in light of the literature, we can identify the following indicators that have the potential to yield valuable results:

1   Perceived effectiveness of communication: how effectively the advertisement communicates;
2   Perceived clarity: whether the advertisement is easy to understand;
3   Referral intention: the potential for the advertisement to generate word of mouth.

Looking at these items it is readily apparent how this kind of diversification can offer a more complete investigation on response to advertising. It comprises a range of instruments that are directly tied to some common goals of marketing campaigns, which are not only aligned with short-term selling objectives but are also meant to capture long-term aims that have to do with generation of income. These objectives and their inclusion into the set of measurements used in research on advertising in multilingual contexts is one of the key advancements of the linguistic approach proposed in this volume. In other words, the employment of linguistic resources in advertising and specifically the choice of one language versus another can be fully connected to indicators that explore more than one goal of advertising. What is the impact of language choice on effectiveness in conveying messages, perceived clarity and referral intention?

4.2 Isolating variables to find response

In order to answer the question above, an experiment involving highly proficient Italian English speakers in Australia was devised. The experiment is a 2 (language of advertisements: English versus Italian) × 2 (language dominance: English versus Italian) between-subject experiment, where multilinguals of Italian descent are presented with stimuli in Italian or in English and then asked to answer questions on them. I have explained how

I set up my experiments on response to advertising in multilingual contexts in another work (Santello 2015). Here I followed exactly that procedure; that is, I recruited 103 men and women above 18 years of age who belong to the Italian community in Australia. The participants were recruited through notices and announcements, invited to a quiet place and randomly assigned to one of the experimental conditions; that is, they did not have the possibility to choose the language in which they were going to see advertisements. Table 4.1 illustrates the distribution of participants across cells and shows the two principal independent variables under scrutiny here: language of advertising and language dominance of the audience.

Among Italian speakers in Australia, language dominance, self-reported and afterwards confirmed like here through the employment of the Gradient Bilingual Dominance Scale (Dunn and Fox Tree 2009), has been shown to "offer adequate information to capture the complexity of their bilingualism and [. . .] describe bilingualism with the consolidation of an individual and a societal perspective" (Santello 2014: 36). This analytical and categorisation instrument is fully consistent with the lived multilingualism described hitherto, in the sense that, while providing a way to divide multilinguals into groups for experimental purposes, it does not disregard key features of their linguistic life (cf. Treffers-Daller 2011) such as amount of use for each language, age of acquisition and changing patterns of language use throughout the lifetime. I adopt here an approach that sees multilingualism as a lived experience as explained in Chapter 3, and I use dominance as a syncretic tool that is malleable and yet does not run the risk of underestimating linguistic elements relating to competence, use and language history, i.e. it does not undervalue the societal elements of their multilingualism while encompassing a set of well-defined features. Table 4.2, adapted from Santello (2014: 31), illustrates the calculated language dominance for speakers who self-report being dominant in English and those who self-report being dominant in Italian, gauged through the method devised by Dunn and Fox Tree (2009).

Table 4.1 Diagrammatic representation of the cells

26 English dominants (EDs)	25 Italian dominants (IDs)
----------- exposed to -----------	----------- exposed to -----------
Advertising in English (AE)	**Advertising in English (AE)**
26 English dominants (EDs)	26 Italian dominants (IDs)
----------- exposed to -----------	------------ exposed ------------
Advertising in Italian (AI)	**Advertising in Italian (AI)**

Table 4.2 Language dominance

Language dominance	English	Mean			−17.41
		95% confidence Interval for mean	☺ ☹	Lower bound Upper bound	−19.56 −15.67
	Italian	Mean			11.13
		95% confidence Interval for mean	☺ ☹	Lower bound Upper bound	9.69 12.58

The questionnaire for the elicitation of response was built using a set of stimuli that have proved both varied and plausible in this sociolinguistic context, as per Table 4.3 built upon Santello (2015: 105), and are here tested on the variables outlined above. These were all seven-point Likert scales, operationalised with the questions explained in the next section.

The participants were given a booklet in which they found the advertisements followed by a set of questions, and at the end they were asked to fill out the language-related questions designed to verify their dominance. The raw data collected through questionnaires were coded, entered into a database and then elaborated. The vast majority of scores were already precoded in the scales used in the questionnaire, thus they needed only to be entered into the database. This activity was performed manually and then checked several times to minimise typing errors.

To analyse the outcomes of the experiments, I ran analysis of variance (ANOVA) and repeated-measures ANOVA, which are the statistical tests that are suitable for a between-subject design with four cells (see Luna and Peracchio 2001: 292–93; Luna and Peracchio 2005b: 51–53). With these tests I intended to compare the indicators of response to advertising in each experimental condition, thus locating significant differences as a function of the language in which the stimuli were conveyed and the language dominance of the respondents. Before running the tests, I systematically checked normality through histograms and homogeneity of variance through the Levene's test (cf. Larson-Hall 2010: 86–88). Afterwards, I performed the tests by calculating the values of systematic and unsystematic variation and gauging the ratio between them (Field 2005: 323–24). Both variations were calculated, taking into account the sums of means squares of the model and the residual sums of means squares, along with their respective degrees of freedom. For each analysis I also calculated the statistical power.

Table 4.3 Experimental advertisements

	Target	Involvement	Motivations	Benefit	Reason why	Tone of voice	Complexity and elaboration of graphics	Size of body copy	Consistency with advertising in this context
1. Shoes	Young/juvenile	Low	Emotional	Fun	None	Emotional	Medium elaboration	Only slogan and payoff	No ☒
2. Online travel agency	General audience	Low	Emotional	Experience of romance	Characteristics of destinations	Highly emotional	Low elaboration	Limited	Yes ☑
3. Furniture	General audience/ families	High	Rational/ emotional	Quality furniture	Experience and reliability	Rational and plain, focusing on solidity and experience	Low elaboration	Extended	Yes ☑
4. Batteries	Young/ juvenile	Low	Rational	Long-lasting batteries	None	Humorous with use of understatement	High elaboration	Slogan and payoff	No ☒

Repeated-measures ANOVA was performed to analyse the four experimental advertisements considered together (cf. Carroll and Luna 2011: 78–80). The indicators of response were taken one by one as dependent variables (see Forehand and Deshpande 2001; Tavassoli and Lee 2003), with language dominance and language of the advertisements as main factors.

Furthermore, I utilised ANOVA to confirm that responses to the four advertisements were statistically different and yet retained the same two-way interaction. I ran the Mauchly's test to check the assumption of sphericity and then corrected the degrees of freedom with Greenhouse-Geisser estimates. After verifying that the four stimuli displayed variability that rendered them significantly different from each other, I ran tests of interaction for the differences among the four advertisements and the two main factors to gauge whether the differences were due to the factors.

4.3 How experiments shed light on advertising in multilingual contexts

The first ANOVA was run on the variable called *perceived effectiveness of communication*. This indicator takes into account how subjects assess the communication act put in place by a specific advertisement, and thus represents a somewhat overall indicator of response in the recipient's judgment. It has been measured through agreement with the statement "the advertisement communicates effectively" represented on a seven-point scale.

The results show the statistical significance of the two factors combined, $F(1, 99) = 14.39$, $p < .01$, $\omega = .96$. When asked to report their assessment of how efficiently the advertisements communicate, EDs[1] indicate AI as more able to communicate effectively (M = 4.37) than AE (M = 3.99). Conversely, among IDs an enhanced perceived effectiveness of communication is connected to advertisements in English (M = 4.43) as opposed to Italian (M = 3.32). In other words, perceived effectiveness differs significantly as a function of both language dominance and language of advertising (see Figure 4.1).

The graph reported above shows the differential influence of the effect, which is more pronounced among IDs than among EDs. The mean difference between the advertisements in Italian and English is 0.38 for EDs and 1.11 for IDs. This latter difference seems particularly marked, which indicates that IDs find advertisements conveyed in English much more effective than their Italian counterparts.

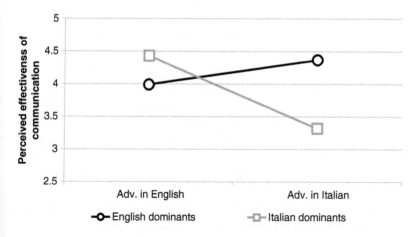

Figure 4.1 Effect of experimental manipulation on perceived effectiveness of communication

The second indicator of response taken into consideration was *perceived clarity*, which gauges the extent to which the advertisement presented appears understandable to the subjects. It was elicited using the question "how easy was it to understand the advertisement?" and measured along a scale which had at its two extremes 'very easy' and 'very difficult'. As previously discussed, perceived clarity is an important factor broadly used in assessing advertising. On perceived clarity ANOVA shows that the effect among EDs of the two experimental variables on this indicator is non-significant [$p > .05$]. The mismatched effect is not applicable to perceived clarity, as the multilinguals who took part in this study judged AE and AI easy or difficult to understand to the same extent. The analysis of this outcome indicates that no enhanced clarity is provided by either language, irrespective of the language dominance of respondents.

This result seems consistent with the linguistic features of the sample in that the participants, albeit characterised by distinct dominance, display differences in their linguistic profile that do not entail any enhanced ease in understanding advertising engendered by language choice. This indicator of response, therefore, seems to confirm that ease of processing effects do not occur among these multilinguals, and thus the language effect found here stems from other factors. I discuss these factors when I present the results on the relationship between language attitudes and response in the next chapter.

I proceeded with the analysis by looking at the item devised to elicit behavioural intentions. This is *referral intention*, i.e. the ability of the advertisement to generate word of mouth. It is a relevant indicator of response as referral is one important goal of advertising as part of a marketing strategy. For instance, word of mouth amplifies the effect of an advertising campaign and generally improves the performance of a brand in the market, for it is able to take a campaign beyond its perceived source and thus contribute to more long-lasting and comprehensive commercial outcomes. Here it was measured in terms of agreement with the statement "I would probably tell others about the company" on a seven-point scale. ANOVA confirms that EDs are more likely to tell others about an advertisement if that advertisement is written in Italian rather than in English. The same pattern occurs among IDs, who are more likely to start word of mouth when the advertisements are in English than when they are in Italian. There exists, hence, a mismatched effect of the language of advertising, in that the least dominant of the two languages is able to engender higher referral intention among multilinguals. Remarkably, scores associated with this item seem to be rather low, with means ranging between 2.74 and 3.67, signifying that these multilinguals do not show an overall propensity to generate word of mouth with regard to these advertisements. Nevertheless, the effect of the two independent variables remains statistically significant, $F(1, 99) = 10.17$, $p < .01$, $\omega = .88$. Advertising seen in the non-dominant language is more likely to engender the promoting effect of word of mouth than the reverse.

The two lines in Figure 4.2 trace the mismatched effect found with regard to referral intention. The influence of the effect is slightly more marked among IDs than among EDs. The language effect in this indicator thus largely confirms the pattern that has been outlined for the other indicators, showing in addition that the effect is extended to behaviour-related variables as well as to evaluative ones.

To sum up, the analyses presented above have shown a mismatched two-way interaction between language dominance and language of advertising in relation to the following variables: perceived effectiveness of communication and referral intention. Overall, Italian English speakers respond more favourably to advertisements in their least dominant language, and this mismatched effect operates in relation to more than one indicator of response, including the behavioural item referral intention. This means that the outcome of the language effect is not to be confined to evaluation but can be more broadly generalised. Interestingly, however, the interaction of the two independent variables does not bring about any consequence on

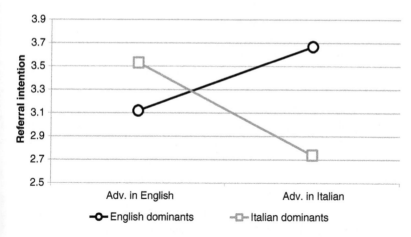

Figure 4.2 Effect of experimental manipulation on referral intention

perceived clarity of messages. In Chapter 5 I will argue that this outcome can be explained not only in light of specific characteristics of the multilingualism of my participants but also assessing the socio-psychological features associated with Italian and English.

4.4 The work of linguistic resources: Exploding response and seeing the effect of language use

The tensions between the goals of marketing and the multilingualism of audiences emerge clearly when Italian English speakers are placed in an experimental situation and asked to judge advertisements. It is evident that response to messages in different languages is driven by the features of the multilingualism that the audiences experience in their lives. In this case the profile of a multilingual group in a local linguistic environment, encapsulated as language dominance, determines the ways in which the group responds to languages as used in messages. Choosing a language means therefore relating to audiences by virtue of the fact that the audiences know that language in a specific way, and that knowledge shapes the 'interaction' (Pisanty and Pellerey 2004) between messages and their recipients.

In the context analysed here, audiences respond more positively to messages conveyed in their least dominant language, but not equally across all indicators. While we can identify a mismatched effect of the language of advertising vis-à-vis language dominance as a general pattern of response, the consideration of individual items of response allows us to establish a clearer link between advertising goals and language effects. In particular, I have noted that the interaction between language dominance and language of advertising brings about statistically significant effects on measures such as perceived effectiveness of communication and referral intention. Notwithstanding this, perceived clarity of advertisements does not differ according to the language in which messages are conveyed, nor does it interact with the multilingualism of the audience, or at least not so much to engender more or less positive response. I will elucidate on what lies behind some of these patterns in the next chapter – where it will be clear that the direct experiences with languages in society are key factors – but here it is important to highlight how the consideration of the range of objectives that campaigns aim at and their intersection with textual strategies, in conjunction with the multilingualism of the audience, are far from being straightforward.

In Chapter 3 multilinguals were conscious of the intricacy associated with the plurality of goals of advertising and were able to position themselves in relation to them. Here through experiments we note that it is in actual fact by breaking up the different indicators that we can further appreciate the composite nature of response and attempt to ascertain how the interaction between messages and audiences comes to be through and thanks to language use. Similarly, it is by means of a reliable and comprehensive appraisal of the multilingualism of the audience, one that takes into account their linguistic profile, that such results can be obtained. Furthermore, consistent with what I have argued in Chapter 2, the goals of advertising and how they are conveyed seem a major node in the work of persuasive communication in multilingual contexts, brought to the surface in its more specific components by a linguistic approach such as the one exposed here, which incorporates experimental setups involving groups of speakers.

The appreciation of the variability of language effects and, in particular, how they fluctuate depending on response indicators itemising marketing points provides an alternative perspective on advertising in multilingual contexts. Not only does it place at the centre the multilingual repertoires of audiences and the way in which they are affected by the use of known linguistic resources in advertising, but it also puts the accent on the marketing side of response. What might emerge is also the fruitfulness of employing multiple items of response, which help to paint a wider and more composite picture of the actual links between language use and the achievement of advertising outcomes. Advertising in multilingual contexts under this perspective is connected with commercial results and is able to raise questions related to the consequences of linguistic choices for the achievement of explicit goals. This is arguably a possible starting point for the complementation of what has been established in terms of textual construction and could potentially lead to a more accurate evaluation of where and how linguistic resources could exert their influence in concrete situations.

Note

1 EDs = English Dominants
   IDs = Italian Dominants
   AE = Advertising in English
   AI = Advertising in Italian

References

Carroll, Ryall, and David Luna. 2011. The Other Meaning of Fluency: Content Accessibility and Language in Advertising to Bilinguals. *Journal of Advertising* 40: 73–84.

Dunn, Alexandra N., and Jean E. Fox Tree. 2009. A Quick, Gradient Bilingual Dominance Scale. *Bilingualism: Language and Cognition* 12: 273–89.

Field, Andy. 2005. *Discovering Statistics Using Spss*. London: Sage.

Forehand, Mark R., and Rohit Deshpande. 2001. What We See Makes Us Who We Are: Priming Ethnic Self-Awareness and Advertising Response. *Journal of Marketing Research (JMR)* 38: 336–48.

Larson-Hall, Jennifer. 2010. *A Guide to Doing Statistics in Second Language Research Using Spss*. New York: Routledge.

Luna, David, and Laura Peracchio. 2001. Moderators of Language Effects in Advertising to Bilinguals: A Psycholinguistic Approach. *Journal of Consumer Research* 28: 284–95.

Luna, David, and Laura Peracchio. 2005a. Advertising to Bilingual Consumers: The Impact of Code-Switching on Persuasion. *Journal of Consumer Research* 31: 760–65.

Luna, David, and Laura Peracchio. 2005b. Sociolinguistic Effects on Code-Switched Ads Targeting Bilingual Consumers. *Journal of Advertising* 34: 43–56.

Pisanty, Valentina, and Roberto Pellerey. 2004. *Semiotica e Interpretazione*. Milan: Bompiani.

Santello, Marco. 2014. Exploring the Bilingualism of a Migrant Community through Language Dominance. *Australian Review of Applied Linguistics* 37: 24–42.

Santello, Marco. 2015. Advertising to Italian English Bilinguals in Australia: Attitudes and Response to Language Selection. *Applied Linguistics* 36: 95–120.

Tavassoli, Nader T., and Yih Hwai Lee. 2003. The Differential Interaction of Auditory and Visual Advertising Elements with Chinese and English. *Journal of Marketing Research (JMR)* 40: 468–80.

Treffers-Daller, Jeanine. 2011. Operationalizing and Measuring Language Dominance. *International Journal of Bilingualism* 15: 147–63.

5 Advertisements in different languages and the role of language attitudes

5.1 Finding what lies behind response

The previous chapter has explored the ways in which advertising is related to specific marketing objectives as a function of the language chosen to convey messages and the linguistic make-up of the audience. By and large Italian English speakers tend to respond in a more favourable manner to advertising written in their least dominant language, even though such response varies when different indicators are used. Arguably, the ensuing pattern points to the necessity of encompassing a range of marketing goals in relation to advertising in multilingual contexts, but the question remains as to what can possibly drive this kind of response. Is there an underlying force that drives this general mismatched response?

In the work that first identified mismatched language effects among multilinguals in terms of advertising evaluation and product evaluation it has been contended that the effect could be linked to "non-fluency related elements, connected to the specific multilingual–multicultural background of Italian English speakers, may have the power to generate the mismatched effect" (Santello 2015a: 115), consistent with socio-psychological features of languages. In this chapter I will build upon those results and particularise those claims by looking into the possible role of language attitudes.

I have discussed extensively in Chapter 1 that advertising is intertwined with market-driven forces that attach symbolic and socio-psychological values to languages. These forces are likely to operate effectively by virtue of the pre-existing linguistic resources that audiences have and can use to decode messages. To supplement this, in Chapter 2 I suggested that both monolingual and codeswitched messages derive their persuasive power from their success in taking into consideration language dynamics in the everydayness of multilingual audiences. In addition, it is useful to remember that early studies have tentatively underlined that language attitudes can be the possible driving energy behind the effectiveness of language choice (Koslow, Shamdasani and Touchstone 1994) and even types of codeswitched slogans (Bishop and Peterson 2011). Nonetheless, previous attempts to connect language attitudes and advertising have been only indicative rather than conclusive, partly because they did not show enough consideration for the localised nature of attitudes (Edwards 1985; 1999), their ties with multilingualism (Lambert 1977) and, crucially, their being made up of a number of different dimensions.

Italian English speakers in Australia display a pattern of language attitudes that is characterised by the concurrent presence of three dimensions: 1) superiority, 2) attractiveness, and 3) efficiency (Santello 2015b). Attractiveness refers to the aesthetic attributes of languages, the range of features that render them pleasant and attractive. Superiority is the dimension that refers to the perceived position and prestige of a language in comparison to another. Efficiency is related to the languages being efficient instruments of communication. These dimensions are formed as a result of constant comparisons between Italian and English, and they are highly idiosyncratic, i.e. localised in this particular sociolinguistic context.

In this chapter I verify whether different ratings on each of the dimensions for English and Italian are in any way related to response to advertising conveyed in those languages. In other words, I test whether the pattern of language attitudes that the two groups of multilinguals display is consistent with the entire pattern of response to Italian and English in advertising. In doing so I intend to establish a relationship between the specific socio-psychological features of the two languages and response to advertising among Italian English speakers.

5.2 Rating English and Italian

In order to elicit attitudes toward Italian and English according to the three dimensions that are germane to this specific speech community, the same participants who were asked to look at the advertisements explained in the previous chapter were also asked to fill out two semantic differentials (Osgood, Suci and Tannenbaum 1957), one for English and one for Italian. The semantic differential comprised the following adjectival pairs, the order of which was randomised: 1) attractiveness (ugly–beautiful, unpleasant–pleasant, cold–warm, unmusical–musical, sour–sweet and unpoetic–poetic); 2) superiority (unimportant–important, poor–rich, useless–useful, worthless – valuable);

3) and efficiency (abstract–contextual, inefficient–efficient, difficult–easy, impractical–practical). An overall score for each of the three dimensions was then calculated for the two languages separately by calculating means. These specific dimensions have been explained in Santello (2015b), where it was clarified how each adjectival pair and its inclusion into each dimension was ascertained through a multi-stage qualitative and quantitative assessment (*ibid*: 13–15).

I first performed the analysis of attitudes toward English by dividing the sample according to dominance (cf. Chapter 4), in order to establish how different multilinguals evaluate the languages across the three dimensions. The data are displayed graphically in Figure 5.1.

When analysing the dimension of *Attractiveness* in relation to English, it is apparent that both English dominants (EDs) and Italian dominants (IDs) express similar attitudes. On a scale from one to seven, EDs rate English 4.08 and IDs rate it 4.09. Independent t-test confirms that there is no significant difference between the two groups [p > .05]. The Attractiveness of English is therefore similarly moderate in both EDs and IDs. Also in terms of *Superiority* of English the two groups display comparable attitudes [p > .05]. However, in this case ratings are higher for both EDs (M = 5.86) and IDs (M = 5.79). This result indicates that English is considered by these multilinguals as a high-status language, irrespectively of their language dominance. However, while along Attractiveness and Superiority language dominance does not create significant distinctions, when considering *Efficiency*, the data present a different picture. In this case EDs rate

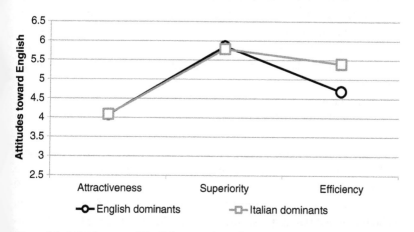

Figure 5.1 Attitudes toward English across Attractiveness, Superiority and Efficiency

English lower (M = 4.69) than IDs (M = 5.40). This difference is significant t(101) = −3.38, p < .01. In other words, English is evaluated as more efficient by multilinguals who are dominant in Italian than by those who are dominant in English.

These results therefore show that English is considered equally by EDs and IDs in terms of Attractiveness and Superiority, but the language is judged as more efficient by IDs than by EDs. It is not within the scope of this monograph to explain the 'contextual antecedents' (Kormos, Kiddle and Csizér 2011: 509) of these ratings, but it is likely that different efficiency ratings in the two groups of multilinguals may be caused by the different settings of acquisition of English. In the case of EDs, English has been acquired in early childhood and then improved and perfected in educational settings. On the contrary, IDs are more likely to be late multilinguals who have acquired English later in life, mainly in interactions with English speakers (Santello 2014: 31–32). It is possible, therefore, that IDs consider English more efficient because it is connected to its practical and contextual use in Australia and less associated with the image of an abstract and difficult language. On the contrary, EDs have studied English for years in school, and this may have contributed to its evaluation as a more difficult and abstract language, connected, for instance, also to domains of use far from everyday interaction, such as literature or science. My results regarding attitudes toward English would then be consistent with those obtained among other groups of Italians in Australia (e.g. Rubino and Bettoni 1990; Bettoni and Rubino 1996; Bettoni and Rubino 1998), where English has been found to enjoy positive evaluations. Overall it is clear not only that English is regarded highly among multilinguals but also that English is evaluated positively along Attractiveness and Superiority, whereas differences between EDs and IDs can be traced along the dimension of Efficiency, which is related to the practical properties of the language for its speakers.

I analysed attitudes toward Italian following the same procedure; that is, I calculated the means for EDs and IDs separately and then compared the two groups through t-tests.

Similarly to what was noted for English, the analysis of *Attractiveness* of Italian indicates analogous ratings for EDs and IDs. Both parts of the sample consider Italian highly attractive. In particular, EDs rate Italian 6.09 and IDs rate it 6.30. The Attractiveness of Italian is therefore equally high in both EDs and IDs, as t-tests show no significant difference [p > .05]. Statistical tests run on the dimension of *Superiority* also reveal no significant difference between the two groups [p > .05]. EDs rate Italian 5.49 and IDs rate the language 5.75. In other words, Italian is evaluated favourably in terms of Superiority by both multilinguals who are dominant in English and those who are dominant in Italian. The data denote the high status of Italian regardless of the dominance of respondents. The examination of *Efficiency* ratings for Italian, on the contrary, suggests differences according to dominance. Specifically, EDs consider Italian moderately efficient (M = 4.46), whereas IDs less so (M = 3.90). The t-test confirms that the difference is significant: $t(101) = 3.61$, $p < .01$. Both groups of multilinguals consider Italian efficient to a moderate extent, but those who are dominant in English tend to rate the language higher along this dimension than do their Italian dominant counterparts.

These results show that Italian is considered equally by EDs and IDs in terms of Attractiveness and Superiority. Conversely, it is judged as more efficient by EDs than by IDs. This outcome can again be justified with the fact that the dimension of Efficiency comprises traits that have to do with the language being contextual and practical. Different ratings are likely to be affected by the different settings of acquisition and use of the language. In the case of IDs, Italian has been acquired in early childhood and then improved and perfected in school. On the contrary, EDs are more likely to have acquired Italian in the home domain, mainly in interactions with Italian speakers and only partly in educational settings. It is possible, therefore, that EDs consider Italian more efficient because it is connected to its practical use in their sociolinguistic environment. On the contrary, IDs have studied Italian in educational settings, as well as having acquired it in other domains. It is possible that education in Italian might have helped to create associations with the language that are more linked to its abstract qualities, although this inference would need to be confirmed with further research.

In sum, EDs and IDs display similar attitudes toward Italian along Attractiveness, rated high, and Superiority, rated high alike. On the contrary, the analysis of Efficiency indicates that EDs rate Italian higher than IDs, which may be due to dissimilarities in how and where the language has been acquired. These multilinguals confirm the position of Italian as a high language, in keeping with findings on trilinguals (see, for instance, Bettoni 1991; Rubino 1993). Moreover, they highlight that discrepancies among different groups of multilinguals do not occur along dimensions of Attractiveness and Superiority but exclusively on the dimension of Efficiency (see Figure 5.2 on p.74).

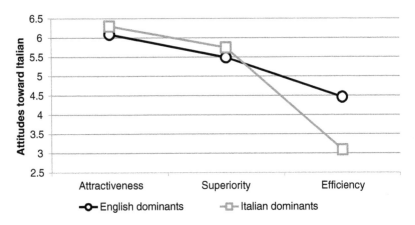

Figure 5.2 Attitudes toward Italian across Attractiveness, Superiority and Efficiency

5.3 Language attitudes and response to advertising

Is there any relationship between this pattern of language attitudes and how multilinguals respond to advertising? If patterns of response and patterns of attitudes were to be connected, this would constitute an important link between the standing of languages in speakers' lives and how, as audiences, multilinguals can be reached by advertising. Therefore, here I seek to verify whether general patterns of response that parallel the language dominance of the subjects can be linked to specific patterns of language attitudes. In particular, the research hypothesis to be verified is the following: is the effect of language dominance over response to advertisements consistent with differences in attitudes to languages between EDs and IDs? Do attitudes toward English have a positive correlation with response to AE and, likewise, do attitudes to Italian have a positive correlation with response to AI?

As outlined above, when analysing the correlation between language dominance and language attitudes, I found both convergent and divergent patterns of response. Crucially I noticed one clear mismatched pattern of relationship between attitudes and language dominance: the attitudes concerning the dimension of Efficiency. Efficiency again is the dimension of language attitudes that comprises the following pairs of adjectives: Abstract–Contextual, Inefficient–Efficient, Difficult–Easy and Impractical–Practical. It is akin to what has been extensively investigated in psycholinguistics (e.g. Gergle, Kraut and Fussell 2004) and refers to the perceived property of language as being an efficient carrier of information (Santello 2015b). A negative correlation between dominance and Efficiency emerges clearly from the data since EDs tend to consider Italian more efficient than English and IDs tend to consider English more efficient. This occurrence is confirmed not only by point-biserial correlations but also by the Pearson correlation test between Efficiency of Italian, Efficiency of English, the difference between the two and language dominance, as shown in Table 5.1.

Table 5.1 shows 1) dominance, which, as discussed in Chapter 3 and Chapter 4, refers to how much a speaker leans toward one language, where values below zero signify English dominance and values above zero indicate Italian dominance; 2) the extent to which English is considered efficient; 3) the extent to which Italian is considered efficient; and 4) the difference between Efficiency ratings of English and Efficiency ratings of Italian. The data indicate that the more a speaker is English dominant, the more likely s/he is to consider Italian more efficient and English less so. Likewise, the more a speaker is Italian dominant, the more likely s/he is to consider English more efficient and Italian less so. The correlation with the difference between Efficiency of English and Efficiency of Italian further confirms such relationship.

It is readily apparent that this mismatch is the same as the one found in response to advertising after variable manipulation. Table 5.2 displays these similarities.

Table 5.1 Correlations between Dominance and Efficiency

		Efficiency – English	Efficiency – Italian	Efficiency – Difference between English and Italian
Language Dominance	Pearson correlation	.389**	−.287**	−.431**
	Sig. (2-tailed)	.001	.003	.001
	N	103	102	102
Efficiency – English	Pearson correlation	1	−.226*	
	Sig. (2-tailed)		0.22	
	N	103	102	
Efficiency – Italian	Pearson correlation	−.226*	1	
	Sig. (2-tailed)	0.22		
	N	102	103	

*Correlation is significant at the .05 level (2-tailed).
**Correlation is significant at the .05 level (2-tailed).

Table 5.2 Schematic representation of correlations between Response to advertising and Efficiency

English scores low on Efficiency	English scores high on Efficiency
Lower Response to Advertising in English	Higher Response to Advertising in English
Italian scores high on Efficiency	Italian scores low on Efficiency
Higher Response to Advertising in Italian	Lower Response to Advertising in Italian

It is therefore reasonable to argue that the variation in response to advertising in all experimental conditions is consistent with the variation in Efficiency occurring in the sample. The two trends may thus be related; that is, the language considered more efficient is the language that engenders more positive response to advertising. Although the Pearson correlation test does not permit to postulate a cause-effect relationship between Efficiency and response to advertising, the co-occurrence of higher and lower scores, as shown in Table 5.2, is consistent with the conclusion that higher efficiency ratings of a language are associated with the power of that language to bring about more favourable response to advertising.

With regard to the research question, it is possible to conclude that:

•   The effect of language dominance over response to advertisements is consistent with difference in attitudes to languages between EDs and IDs;
•   Attitudes toward English have a positive correlation with response to AE and, likewise, attitudes to Italian have a positive correlation with response to AI. This correlation occurs exclusively for the dimension of Efficiency.

The research hypothesis is thus confirmed and, specifically, finds experimental support for one particular dimension, i.e. that of Efficiency. In this context the perceived ability of a language to be efficient is the dimension of attitudes that holds a prominent role. In other words, these multilinguals perceive their languages at different levels of Efficiency, and this seems to be related to the way in which they respond to advertising in these languages. This result is in keeping with what emerged in Chapter 3, where multilinguals were shown to tap into their direct experiences with the languages to form their attitudes to languages in advertising. Participants were able to acknowledge the conflicting trajectories of languages in multilingual lives as well as the languages' socio-psychological attributes. Specifically, declarative data indicated that attitudes to languages in advertising are paired with the capability of the language to convey messages to specific audiences, which is a point that finds particularisation in these experiments. Here the results reveal that the attributes of the languages that render them capable carriers of communication converge toward the dimension of Efficiency. That is to say, attitudes to languages and, more exactly, Efficiency of English and Italian are related to the languages' capability of communicating in an effective way to target audiences. Once again, this incidence is consistent with the conclusion that superior Efficiency ratings of a language are associated with the power of that language to produce more favourable response.

5.4 From symbolism to attitudinal boost

After verifying that advertising in different languages is decoded by speakers depending on the features of their own linguistic make-up and that different goals of advertising are central informative indicators, this chapter aimed to find out what lies behind these processes. Through a multidimensional elicitation of language attitudes it was possible to show that this specific group of multilinguals shows a pattern of attitudes that varies as a function of language dominance, but only in terms of efficiency of the languages. This was then shown to be consistent with response to messages, establishing a neat co-occurrence of high efficiency ratings of a language and positive response to advertising in that language.

This finding constitutes an unprecedented association between mismatched patterns of response and language attitudes. The role played by this dimension of language attitudes can be explained in light of the centrality of non-fluency-related variables in moderating response to advertising. Specifically, these data lend support to studies that have found consequences of socio-psychological attributes of languages to advertising in multiple languages, and studies that established the importance of language attitudes in moderating language effects in advertising to multilinguals, as discussed in both Chapter 1 and Chapter 2.

More broadly, this result offers additional validation to the corpus of research on multilingualism in advertising, where the socio-psychological attributes of languages have been found to play a crucial role in how languages function in advertising. Tej Bhatia and William Ritchie (2006), for instance, have argued that languages in advertising are associated with particular socio-psychological features, by virtue of which different languages are employed in advertising (cf. also Santello 2015a). Their analysis of advertising texts, which shows strong commonalities with a number of other studies as argued in Chapter 2, finds in the present research grounds of substantiation from the perspective of the audience's response to messages. Furthermore, these data indicate that, among multilinguals, the socio-psychological features of languages are linked specifically to language attitudes.

With regard to studies on advertising to multilingual speakers, these outcomes add validity to the few studies that have addressed the role of language attitudes in prompting language effects in advertising. In particular, the pioneering study by Koslow, Shamdasani and Touchstone (1994) proposed that language attitudes were responsible for the different response of Spanish English multilinguals toward languages in advertising. In a similar fashion, Luna and Peracchio (2005) established a link between the evaluation of slogans and language attitudes, arguing that majority languages are associated with more positive concepts, such as progress, education and integration, whereas minority languages elicit marginalisation, discrimination and a feeling of inferiority (Luna 2004: 150). The positive or negative evaluation associated with a language would be transferred into the evaluation of the slogan as a whole. It is important therefore to acknowledge that the research conducted on multilinguals in the US was ground-breaking in underscoring the significance that these socio-psychological elements have in advertising to multilinguals, although it could only be considered indicative of the actual role of language attitudes, as their measures (e.g. perceived friendliness, convincing ability and influence of languages) did not find antecedents in contemporary language attitude research. On the contrary, the present study has explored language attitudes from a perspective that takes into account the specific language attitudes in literature (Santello 2015b). In particular, the exploration of attitudes' multidimensionality has afforded the possibility to identify the exact dimension that matches response to advertising. This conclusion therefore takes further the suggestions made by Koslow and colleagues and creates a link between one specific dimension of language attitudes and response to advertising.

In order to understand the hidden processes that are at play when advertising involves multilingualism, it is valuable to go deeper into the mechanisms that connect the use of linguistic resources in messages, the reaction of audiences and how such reaction is, in turn, associated with the relationships audiences have built with their own linguistic repertoires. In Chapter 2 and Chapter 3 it was stressed that this relationship is by no means straightforward or even steady over time. However, language attitudes research offers the tools to capture value judgements that partly account for such relationship (Garrett 2010), provided that the complex multidimensionality of language attitudes is correctly extracted and analysed (Baker 1992; 2009). Once attitudes to languages are measured in conjunction with response to advertising that employs those languages, a clearer picture of what underpins the work of languages can arise. The picture may contribute to the description of what forces may drive response away from expected associations between linguistic abilities in one language and advertising constructed through that language. Among these forces, something charges languages with a form of persuasive power, and language attitudes seem to be able to point toward undercurrents that are by and large consistent with what happens at a discursive level. The present study delving into languages as symbolic enhancers connects their meaning-making to the work of socio-psychological attributes. These attributes are, again, clearly aligned with the dimensions of language attitudes that stem from the lived experience of multilinguals and how they create a relationship with their linguistic resources. In other words, the 'multilingual reality' (cf. also Heugh 2000) of audiences and the corresponding complex pattern of attitudes to languages may be thought of as the basis of the communication that advertising establishes through different codes. Complementing the advancements outlined in the previous chapters, this additional step provides further elements for an understanding of the interconnections between linguistic resources, languages charged with localised connotations within a group of speakers and the functioning of languages in marketing communication.

References

Baker, Colin. 1992. *Attitudes and Language*. Clevedon: Multilingual Matters.

Baker, Colin. 2009. Survey Methods in Researching Language and Education. In Nancy H. Hornberger (ed.) *Encyclopedia of Language and Education*. Berlin: Springer. 35–46.

Bettoni, Camilla. 1991. Language Variety among Italians: Anglicisation, Attrition and Attitudes. In Suzanne Romaine (ed.) *Language in Australia*. Cambridge: Cambridge University Press. 263–69.

Bettoni, Camilla, and Antonia Rubino. 1996. *Emigrazione e Comportamento Linguistico: Un'indagine sul Trilinguismo dei Siciliani e dei Veneti in Australia*. Galatina: Congedo.

Bettoni, Camilla, and Antonia Rubino. 1998. Language Maintenance and Language Shift: Dialect Vs Italian among Italo-Australians. *Australian Review of Applied Linguistics* 21: 21–39.

Bhatia, Tej K., and William C. Ritchie. 2006. Bilingualism in the Global Media and Advertising. In Tej K. Bhatia and William C. Ritchie (eds.) *The Handbook of Bilingualism*. Malden, MA: Blackwell Publishing. 513–16.

Bishop, Melissa, and Mark Peterson. 2011. Comprende Code Switching? Young Mexican-Americans' Responses to Language Alternation in Print Advertising. *Journal of Advertising Research* 51: 648–59.

Edwards, John. 1985. *Language, Society and Identity*. Oxford: Blackwell Publishing.

Edwards, John. 1999. Refining Our Understanding of Language Attitudes. *Journal of Language and Social Psychology* 15: 101–10.

Garrett, Peter. 2010. *Attitudes to Language*. Cambridge: Cambridge University Press.

Gergle, Darren, Robert E. Kraut, and Susan R. Fussell. 2004. Language Efficiency and Visual Technology – Minimizing Collaborative Effort with Visual Information. *Journal of Language and Social Psychology* 23: 491–517.

Heugh, Kathleen. 2000. Multilingual Voices – Isolation and the Crumbling of Bridges. *Agenda* 16: 21–33.

Kormos, Judit, Thom Kiddle, and Kata Csizér. 2011. Systems of Goals, Attitudes, and Self-Related Beliefs in Second-Language-Learning Motivation. *Applied Linguistics* 23: 495–516.

Koslow, Scott, Prem N. Shamdasani, and Ellen E. Touchstone. 1994. Exploring Language Effects in Ethnic Advertising: A Sociolinguistic Perspective. *Journal of Consumer Research* 20: 575–85.

Lambert, Wallace E. 1977. Measurement of the Linguistic Dominance of Bilinguals. In P. Hornby (ed.) *Bilingualism: Psychological, Social and Educational Implications*. New York: Academic Press. 15–27.

Luna, David. 2004. Language Processing, Affect, and Cognition: Word and Sentence Structure Effects across Languages. *Advances in Consumer Research* 31: 148–51.

Luna, David, and Laura Peracchio. 2005. Sociolinguistic Effects on Code-Switched Ads Targeting Bilingual Consumers. *Journal of Advertising* 34: 43–56.

Osgood, Charles E., J. Suci Suci, and Percy H. Tannenbaum. 1957. *The Measurement of Meaning*. Urbana: University of Illinois Press.

Rubino, Antonia. 1993. From Trilingualism to Monolingualism: A Case Study of Language Shift in a Sicilian-Australian Family. PhD Thesis. Sydney: The University of Sydney.

Rubino, Antonia, and Camilla Bettoni. 1990. The Use of English among Italo-Australians in Sydney. *Australian Review of Applied Linguistics* 14: 58–89.

Santello, Marco. 2014. Exploring the Bilingualism of a Migrant Community through Language Dominance. *Australian Review of Applied Linguistics* 37: 24–42.

Santello, Marco. 2015a. Advertising to Italian English Bilinguals in Australia: Attitudes and Response to Language Selection. *Applied Linguistics* 36: 95–120.

Santello, Marco. 2015b. Bilingual Idiosyncratic Dimensions of Language Attitudes. *International Journal of Bilingual Education and Bilingualism* 18: 1–25.

Conclusion

This body of work is devoted to proposing a way to explore advertising in conjunction with multilingualism that gives prominence to linguistic resources considered as both strategic tools for marketing communication and as part of audiences' repertoires. Taking as a departure point the positions supported in many great writings on the symbolic and socio-psychological work of languages, as well as on their being linked to psycholinguistic routes to persuasion, in this volume I tested the heuristic virtues of a linguistic approach that emphasises response. The proposition is that observing multilingual audiences when they decode messages can produce a wealth of data that can differentiate explicitly the factors that are responsible for effective communication and pose new broader questions.

In fact the previous chapters have tried to shed light on advertising in relation to multilingualism as it moves from using a multiplicity of linguistic resources in building texts to taking into account the resources that pertain to 'the bi-multilingual existence' (Kelly-Holmes 2005: 173) of the addressee of advertising. We are still far away from a full understanding of the complexity of the tensions between the use of specific varieties in advertising and their actual relationship with the multilingualism of the audience. What we do know is that there is a fissure – at least in terms of power dynamics – between the linguistic strategies that underlie advertising campaigns and the kind of multilingualism that audiences may experience in their lives. Advertising's multilingualism is rooted in the mediascape and, as such, does not mirror or represent the use of languages in the daily settings where they are imbued with localised trajectories of meaning-making (Bhatia 2000; Bhatia and Ritchie 2006). Yet, in this volume I showed that linguistic resources generate meaning in advertising precisely thanks to an intricate relationship with the resources that the recipients are expected to

resort to. It is by virtue of the interplay between the language used in messages and the repertoires of the audience that advertising does what it aims
to do. In other words, advertising in multilingual contexts, despite establishing forms of impersonal bilingualism and language fetish, in actual fact
speaks to societal multilingualism.

In this volume I chose to look at advertising from the side of the audience,
delving into the decoding practices they display through declarative data
and, subsequently, engaging with the effects of specific linguistic variables
in conjunction with marketing goals. I inquired into the 'context of reception' (Bullo 2014: 40) and built upon the response mechanisms found to be at
play among Hispanics in the US (Koslow, Shamdasani and Touchstone 1994;
Luna and Peracchio 2005; Luna, Ringberg and Peracchio 2008; Carroll and
Luna 2011), where having an understanding of the linguistic reality of the
multilingual speakers that advertising intends to address was found in many
ways imperative to successful communication. Key to my approach is, on
the one hand, the acknowledgement of the complexity of multilingualism –
from which societal dimensions are never erased even when such complexity
has to be computed into variables – and, on the other hand, the multifarious
nature of both marketing goals and attitudes to language.

I have illustrated that multilinguals interact with language use in advertising, voicing their attitudes as shaped by and through lived experiences with
the languages. Their attitudes in interaction are the result of a highly contextualised development where their being touched by languages is re-worked
in light of specific encounters in localised discursive planes. It was noted
that multilinguals hold a nuanced cognisance of the plurality of marketing
factors that underlie advertising campaigns and of the ways in which these
might be intertwined with linguistic strategies. Moreover, it was striking to
observe that data emerged through group interactions can both parallel and
complement textual studies on multilingualism in advertising, while also
building a bridge toward the assessment of response patterns.

Experimental data have been shown to provide fine-grained insights
into the interconnections between languages used in messages, repertoires
and marketing goals. It was possible to find a pattern of response that does
not stem from processing fluency effects, but is powered by the meaning
that language choice engenders. Crucially, the employment of linguistic
resources in advertising – and specifically the choice of one language versus another – is to be fully connected to indicators that explore the goals of
advertising. Among Italian English speakers in Australia we can identify a
mismatched pattern of response where the language in which the audience

is least dominant is capable of producing more positive response, but not in a uniform fashion across indicators of response. Language choice, for instance, does not make an advertisement stand out or enhance its clarity, while it clearly impinges on perceived effectiveness of communication and, interestingly, behavioural propensity to generate word of mouth. The patterns seem to point toward forms of intersection between textual strategies and multilingualism of the audience that remain to be clarified (see also Krishna and Ahluwalia 2008). What is clear is that by breaking up the different indicators of response, we can appreciate the composite nature of response and start to ascertain how the interaction between messages and audiences comes to be through and thanks to language use.

As noted above, one key finding of the present study is that the differential response to advertisements in different languages is not solely driven by language effects linked to ease of processing but also by other language-related features. These features are contiguous to the symbolism and indexical work of languages established in discourse analytical research, but they are expanded and particularised herein in a bid to verify whether language attitudes might be consistent with mismatched patterns of response. This is indeed the case, but a fundamental role is held by only one dimension of language attitudes, the 'efficiency' of languages, i.e. their being considered practical vehicles of meaning. Such consideration, formed in contextualised linguistic environments alongside other dimensions of language attitudes (Santello 2015), accounts for the standing of languages in speakers' lives and how, in turn, multilinguals as audiences can be reached by advertising. This establishes a relationship between specific socio-psychological features of languages, in this case Italian and English among speakers in Australia, and response to advertising. Such relationship constitutes a further element explaining how the multilingual reality of the audiences and the corresponding complex pattern of attitudes to languages can be at the basis of the communication that advertising brings about via different codes.

Multilingual contexts, localised response and their implications

If we consider that the majority of people worldwide are multilingual and that increasing transnational mobility is a factor that enhances and complicates multilingualism, it is not difficult to see how advertising in multilingual contexts may sound almost like a tautology. Advertising nearly inevitably takes shape in sites where languages come into contact and, at the same time, advertising itself has been described as a form of multilingual communication in its essence, due to its tendency to employ extreme forms of multimodality and intricate semiosis (Kelly-Holmes 2005; Martin 2005). Yet it has not gone unnoticed that playing out languages in advertising discourse, however superdiverse it may appear, does not equate to acceptance or even exploitation of societal multilingualism (Kelly-Holmes 2005: 176–78).

Marketers and public-sector players alike, nonetheless, are trying at a progressively faster pace to devise campaigns that are aligned with the multilingualism of the societies in which they operate (Peracchio, Bublitz and Luna 2014: 438–39). The question remains as to how these players are doing so and whether they can see what lies behind multilingualism.

This volume dissected a number of issues that are embedded in advertising and multilingualism, proposing a theoretical and methodological line that harmonises some of the discontinuities in the field. I kept in mind the intricacy of multilingual realities (Grosjean 1982; 2010) by acknowledging specifically their socially situated nature and avoiding the use of linguistic items taken exclusively at an individual level. I also explained the significance of marketing goals at a discursive level as well as – and this is central – at the level of response, thus answering questions relating to language choice in advertising targeting contemporary societies, where multilingual resources are deployed in daily life as well as in mediascapes. In order to do so, this study had to be interdisciplinary in nature and embrace mixed methods. While sitting firmly within multilingualism research, it also builds on the advancements in advertising to multilinguals. The methodological approach combines qualitative and quantitative procedures, thus giving examples of a spectrum of tools that could be used in this kind of research. This has allowed the surfacing of a clear connection between the linguistic repertoires of the audience, their localised attitudes to languages and their response to language strategies in advertising, varying according to a range of marketing objectives.

These results might be informative for advertising professionals who are interested in multilingual target audiences. When implementing the linguistic choices that best serve their purposes, they might want to look at this study as a reference on how multilingual groups respond when reached by campaigns that use their languages. My sample of speakers of Italian and English could potentially be split into two subsegments according to their dominance, in that we know that different dominances and attitudes to language are associated with different responses. Similar choices may be applicable to other groups; specific decisions would depend on the goals that campaigns intend to achieve and how they connect with the linguistic elements relevant to the multilinguals under consideration. In particular, not only their specific multilingualism but also their language attitudes analysed according to their relevant idiosyncratic dimensions are to be verified if attempting to predict patterns of response. On a similar note, the outcomes of this research may also potentially endow the public sector with new data to be taken into consideration when communicating important policies to multilinguals. Conveying messages in the most effective way, including through an appropriate language choice, may contribute to the success of a number of policies, such as those related to health, welfare and social involvement. Yet, practitioners are to be mindful of the fact that we still largely ignore the possible impact of other variables that may be associated, for instance, with product-related or medium-related elements.

Looking ahead

Societies mutate and so do the resources that groups and individuals deploy to make sense of the world both within and without the market sphere. Advertising in multilingual contexts takes ever-changing shapes that, whilst maintaining a number of fixities, also engage with the growing intricacy of social relations globally and locally (Cook 2001; Declercq 2011). In this sense, in advertising too language is "one element in a richer and more faceted configuration of semiotic resources" (Blommaert 2013: 618), where complexity rather than multiplicity dominates. This study has only scratched the surface of such complexity, indicating some patterns that tie linguistic resources and patterns of response, but other fundamental issues remain to be inspected.

Among the questions this research has raised, the relationship between trends involving the exploitation of language in the market and the lived experiences of multilingualism is still an outstanding one. It would appear that the more an advertisement enters into dialogue with local linguistic repertoires, the more this can enhance its chances of success. The research presented has highlighted that this dialogue is indeed prolific, but the terms in which it can be established are underexplored and are arguably bound to show contradictions, if not even structural discrepancies, between different modes whereby resources are mobilised. The extent to which these discrepancies unfold and multiply is a subject that can be surveyed by linguists who are interested in the intervening dynamisms that pull together advertising and language use.

One main area that also awaits exploration is that of translanguaging and advertising. It has been suggested that by mixing linguistic resources advertisements are able to capture "not only the message for bilinguals, but also their hybridity" (Garcia and Li Wei 2014: 23). It would be critical to establish how the creativity and the transformative power of translanguaging (Li Wei 2011: 5–12) reshape not only textual construction but also the very relationship between multilingual audiences and multilingual messages via branding strategies. The existence of different interpretations by different audiences based on their resources is wholly embedded in the notion of translanguaging (Garcia and Li Wei 2014: 32–36), and including additional linguistic items such as syntactic elements (Yorkston and De Mello 2005) or phonemes (Klink 2000) can only enrich the magnitude of this line of research.

Lastly, it would be interesting to undertake an exploration of what occurs at a decision-making level. The examination of what types of resources are taken up at different stages of advertising production – for instance, how copywriters and art designers make use of information from the market, their own personal engagement with language and institutional strategies – is a promising area of inquiry (cf. Thurlow forthcoming). This would open more portals for interdisciplinary efforts, where research strands that are usually marching separately, such as marketing, bilingual cognition, intercultural pragmatics and multilingualism in the workplace, could find common paths.

References

Bhatia, Tej K. 2000. *Advertising in Rural India: Language, Marketing Communication, and Consumerism*. Tokyo: Tokyo Univeristy of Foreign Studies.

Bhatia, Tej K., and William C. Ritchie. 2006. Bilingualism in the Global Media and Advertising. In Tej K. Bhatia and William C. Ritchie (eds.) *The Handbook of Bilingualism*. Malden, MA: Blackwell Publishing. 513–16.

Blommaert, Jan. 2013. Complexity, Accent, and Conviviality: Concluding Comments. *Applied Linguistics* 34: 613–22.

Bullo, Stella. 2014. *Evaluation in Advertising Reception: A Socio-Cognitive and Linguistic Perspective*. Houndsmill: Palgrave Macmillan.

Carroll, Ryall, and David Luna. 2011. The Other Meaning of Fluency: Content Accessibility and Language in Advertising to Bilinguals. *Journal of Advertising* 40: 73–84.

Cook, Guy. 2001. *The Discourse of Advertising*. London: Routledge.

Declercq, Christophe. 2011. Advertising and Localization. In Kirsten Malmkjær and Kevin Windle (eds.) *The Oxford Handbook of Translation Studies*. Oxford; New York: Oxford University Press. 262–74.

Garcia, Ofelia, and Li Wei 2014. *Translanguaging: Language, Bilingualism and Education*. Basingstoke: Palgrave Macmillan.

Grosjean, François. 1982. *Life with Two Languages: An Introduction to Bilingualism*. Cambridge: Harvard University Press.

Grosjean, François. 2010. *Bilingual: Life and Reality*. Cambridge: Harvard University Press.

Kelly-Holmes, Helen. 2005. *Advertising as Multilingual Communication*. Houndmills, Basingstoke, Hampshire: Palgrave Macmillan.

Klink, Richard. 2000. Creating Brand Names with Meaning: The Use of Sound Symbolism. *Marketing Letters* 11: 5–20.

Koslow, Scott, Prem N. Shamdasani, and Ellen E. Touchstone. 1994. Exploring Language Effects in Ethnic Advertising: A Sociolinguistic Perspective. *Journal of Consumer Research* 20: 575–85.

Krishna, Aradhna, and Rohini Ahluwalia. 2008. Language Choice in Advertising to Bilinguals: Asymmetric Effects for Multinationals Versus Local Firms. *Journal of Consumer Research* 35: 692–705.

Li Wei. 2011. Moment Analysis and Translanguaging Space: Discursive Construction of Identities by Multilingual Chinese Youth in Britain. *Journal of Pragmatics* 43: 1222–35.

Luna, David, and Laura Peracchio. 2005. Sociolinguistic Effects on Code-Switched Ads Targeting Bilingual Consumers. *Journal of Advertising* 34: 43–56.

Luna, David, Torsten Ringberg, and Laura Peracchio. 2008. One Individual, Two Identities: Frame Switching among Biculturals. *Journal of Consumer Research* 35: 279–93.

Martin, Elizabeth. 2005. *Marketing Identities through Language: English and Global Imagery in French Advertising*. Basingstoke: Palgrave Macmillan.

Peracchio, Laura, Melissa Bublitz, and David Luna. 2014. Cultural Diversity and Marketing: The Multicultural Consumer. In Verónica Benet-Martínez and Ying-yi Hong (eds.) *The Oxford Handbook of Multicultural Identity*. Oxford: Oxford University Press. 438–61.

Santello, Marco. 2015. Bilingual Idiosyncratic Dimensions of Language Attitudes. *International Journal of Bilingual Education and Bilingualism* 18: 1–25.

Thurlow, Crispin (forthcoming). Critical discourse studies in/of applied contexts: Missed opportunities, fraught possibilities. In John Flowerdew and John Richardson (eds), *The Routledge Handbook of Critical Discourse Analysis*. London: Routledge.

Yorkston, Eric, and Gustavo De Mello. 2005. Linguistic Gender Marking and Categorization. *Journal of Consumer Research* 32: 224–34.

Index

For Product Safety Concerns and Information please contact our EU
representative GPSR@taylorandfrancis.com
Taylor & Francis Verlag GmbH, Kaufingerstraße 24, 80331 München, Germany

www.ingramcontent.com/pod-product-compliance
Ingram Content Group UK Ltd.
Pitfield, Milton Keynes, MK11 3LW, UK
UKHW021420080625
459435UK00011B/90